The Recovery of the True Self

Robert D. Phillips, M.D.

Library of Congress Catalog Card Number 95-68897

ISBN Number 1-57087-147-7

Production design by Robin Ober

Published by *Professional Press*, P.O. Box 4371, Chapel Hill,
NC 27515-4371
                                    for

Medicine Wheel Publications; 206 Ridgecrest Drive,
Chapel Hill, NC   27514

Manufactured in the United States of America
96 95 94 93 92   10 9 8 7 6 5 4 3 2 1

Contents

Also by Robert D. Phillips, M.D.

Structural Symbiotic Systems, 1975

Glossary

ANTHROPOLOGY: The study and the science of the human animal species. Any particular view of the nature of "man" (the human animal, whose paradigmatic gender, ironically, is "woman"). From the Greek: "anthrop," human being; and "logia," reason, knowledge, science.

AUTONOMY: The condition of mature interdependence. The goal of the maturational process. The combination of optimal dependence with optimal independence. Synonymous with "direction by the True Self."

CONTAINER: Common usage: Anything that holds within. Particular usage in my theoretical system: Everything that holds the human animal within. Derived from Donald Winnicott's term, "the maternal holding environment." Successive containers are the uterus, the mother's arms, the Ego, and the concentric environments of society and Nature.

DISCOUNT: Any arbitrary unscientific diminution or reduction of reality. Used in this text especially in reference to diminution of personal worth and capability, one's own or that of another person.

EGO: That visible tangible part of the Person which is "wrapped around" and contains the other part of the Person, called the Self. The Ego is the organ of adaptation which provides communication and commerce between the Person and the environment.

ENVIRONMENT: Term used primarily to refer to everything which surrounds and contains the Person externally from the uterus to the cosmos. Also refers to the internal psychophysiological-electrochemical "space" within the Person, the "space" between the Self and the Ego, the internal environment.

GENERAL SYSTEM THEORY: A scientific philosophy designed to distinguish everything in the universe between vitalistic open-system growth and mechanistic closed-system function.

GESTALT THERAPY: A psychotherapy system devised by Fritz Perls and derived from the academic study of "Gestalt" phenomena. This basic field of academic psychology teaches us that any object ("figure") is perceived differently in different contexts, backgrounds, or frames ("fields" or "grounds"). Gestalt psychology also "explains" our intuitive understanding that "the whole is greater than the sum of the parts."

GRANDIOSITY: Any arbitrary unscientific exaggeration or enlargement of reality. Used in this text especially in reference to denial of personal limitations and capacities, one's own or those of another person.

INDIGENOUS: Native, original, aboriginal. Growing or living naturally in a particular region or environment.

INJUNCTIONS: Orders or admonitions. In the special vocabulary of Eric Berne's system of Transactional Analysis they are parental commands for a child to be certain ways and do certain things that serve the parent's needs. Example: Don't Grow Up or Don't Be Sexual. (COUNTERINJUNCTIONS are parental messages which superficially appear to oppose the INJUNCTIONS but which actually reinforce the prolonged dependency on the self-serving parent. Example: Try Hard or Be Perfect.)

MID-LIFE CRISIS: A vague and mystifying cultural concept which simultaneously recognizes and obscures recognition of the molting re-organization which occurs naturally in the fourth and fifth decades of human development. Crisis means concurrent vulnerability and opportunity; the culture emphasizes the former and psychotherapy the latter.

NARCISSISM: The expressive energy of the Self, or "narcissistic sector" of the Person. Narcissistic energy per se is neither good nor bad; it is amoral, not immoral. The contemporary culture ordinarily speaks of narcissism in a pejorative way. (Refer to Chapter Six: Notes on Narcissism).

OBJECT (OBJECT-RELATING): In the special language of psychoanalytic theory, the word "object" refers to everything outside the subject person, especially other people. In my special language it is the person's Ego which relates to the object-world. The "object-relating sector" is the Ego.

PROVIDING BEHAVIOR: The human animal's procurement activity. The expression of outreach energy into the environment. The activity of the donor.

RECEIVING BEHAVIOR: The human animal's intake activity, following procurement from the environment by one's self or by some other person. The activity of the recipient.

RAPPROCHEMENT: French word meaning "to bring together, especially amongst people." In the special vocabulary of developmental theory it refers to the main psychosocial task of the toddler-age child.

SCRIPT: In the special language of Transactional Analysis the life-plan which is intruded by parents into the child who then incorporates it in the Ego where it operates unconsciously and unnaturally.

SECONDARY GAIN: A benefit secondary, or as a consequence, to a loss or an injury or an illness. In the vernacular, the lemonade one makes from a "lemon" or the purse which one makes from life's sow's ears.

SELF: The soul, the spirit, the essence of the Person. The "nucleus" in my cellular model. The pristine Self is the recoverable True Self.

STEADY-STATE: A generous range adequate for normal functioning in an open system, in contrast to the strict precise homeostatic set-point of a closed system.

SYMBIOTIC: Descriptive of symbiosis, a relationship within which all the participants derive significant, albeit unequal, benefit. For example: a co-dependent interpersonal pair, or a moss which takes sustenance from and gives sustenance to a host tree. Contrasting with a parasitic relationship in which the host provides something but gets nothing in return.

TRANSACTIONAL ANALYSIS: A system of psychotherapeutic theory and practice based on an understanding of the impact of interpersonal transactions, which are specific sequences in on-going interactions or relationships.

TRANSFERENCE: A specific term in psychoanalysis referring to the transfer of historically unconsummated affects, emotions, attitudes, and perceptions onto a contemporary person or situation, most significantly onto the analyst or therapist.
(COUNTERTRANSFERENCE is a term reserved for that process in which the analyst or therapist transfers some unconsummated feelings or perceptions onto the contemporary patient).

Author's Introduction

I'VE KNOWN A FEW "REAL" WRITERS — THOSE BRAVE PEOPLE WHO write for a living as well as for a calling. They tell me that their best stories "write themselves," while they serve as scribes. Their characters appear, unheralded, and introduce themselves when the story needs them.

This book insistently wrote itself, rising from the ashes of two earlier manuscripts which were, like Icarus of old, incinerated by flights of grandiosity. During the fifteen years of abortion and stillbirths and re-fertilizations, this book has patiently taught me. It kept calling for simplicity and paring down, but I continued to think I knew best — I stubbornly fed it crêpes and caviar until it gagged. But faithful like a dog, it stayed with me until I could finally practice what I was preaching.

I was writing about open-systems theory and I knew the terms trial-and-error, false-start, and overshoot, but of my earlier efforts I was more critical and unforgiving, restricting myself to the closed-system requirements of "getting it just right."

Then about four years ago I was introduced to the viable Native American culture. Under the tutelage of wise Indian elders I regained perspective, patience, and the capacity to laugh at myself; consequently there came some vision and creativity. I started writing again, with a lighter heart and a clearer eye.

In fresh and ancient company, I remembered my instructions. I had set out to write for my patients, to leave them reminders of all they had done and of how they had done it. But in those earlier efforts, I was narcissistically stimulated to imagine "my book" becoming a best-seller or a theoretical classic which would refute and convert conservative colleagues to my ways of thinking. I became possessive. It was "my book" to glorify me, instead of "their book" to be transcribed by me. With so much baggage the first two efforts became heavy indeed.

After I began to write more naturally I asked my long-time best-friend Bill Blythe to read the first two chapters. He liked the material and he encouraged me emotionally and substantively. Bill introduced me and the first chapters to Larry Churchill, the highly regarded medical ethicist at the University of North Carolina in Chapel Hill. Larry also was enthusiastic and he recommended several publishing venues.

Bill Blythe said he would like his son Will to take a look at what I was writing. I've known Will since his childhood in Chapel Hill but I had seen little of him since he became literary editor of Esquire Magazine. I jumped at the suggestion and shuttled the first half-dozen chapters to Will, feeling honored but not very expectant. I was delighted shortly to hear Will on the telephone not only approving my work but rejoicing in its message. Will "dug" my material and he has become my main cheerleader, hawker, and conduit to the publishing world in Manhattan.

During that summer of 1994 when the Blythe men were supporting me so stoutly I visited one of our North Carolina beaches. Out for an early morning jog I heard someone call my name from up-strand. I walked over to the caller and recognized her as my high-school teacher of English and journalism, the poet Grace Gibson. We had had a few fleeting contacts in the intervening fifty years but not catch-up talking until that chance meeting at Sunset Beach. Part of my catch-up had to do with the borning book; she wanted to look it over. I sent Grace the manuscript later that week. In a few days she returned it to me as thoroughly analyzed and critiqued as any high school paper from yesteryear. The inveterate and passionate teacher still, Grace had red-marked the glitches, raised tough questions, corrected the punctuation, and supplied a two-page opinion on readability and style! There are lots of ways to recapture one's youth — this was a gracious one.

Will and Grace continue urging me on, ploughing the market soil while I write.

Back in 1992 when I finished the second effort, two literary friends, Rhoda Weyr and Townsend Ludington read the ponderous manuscript. They read independently of each other and their complaints, incisive but gentle, were convincingly in accord with each other. I think I wanted endorsement rather than candor at that point. My anger at those realists has long since been replaced by solid gratitude. And now when I re-read Tome I and Tome II I am more amused than embarrassed.

Less immediately but more continually my principal colleague in developing the "cellular model" (which is the theoretical centerpiece of this book) has been Denton Roberts from Los Angeles. Denton organized a study-group of psychotherapists in southern California over twenty years ago. The group has continued across those years and I have been invited a dozen times to do workshops for them; sometimes we met in the city, sometimes in the Sierra backcountry. I recall that Denton and I were slaking our thirst at an unpretentious Mountainside tavern when I drew the first cellular model on a paper napkin. The original washed away in Denton's spilt beer, but many generations of revisions have followed. Denton's training was in theology and mine in biology. Our pursuit of the True Self has been complementary.

At the suggestion of Grace Gibson, my erstwhile English teacher, I am providing a GLOSSARY. "Make it as easy for them as you can," she said. I have put it in the front of the book, alongside the other introductions.

The four life-stories in the text are essentially fictional amalgams about two men and two women. I have myself been in and out of therapy for many years, so it was obvious that the four stories are internally *autobiographical.* We are, indeed, all connected.

The last and un-least of my friends to introduce is Marianne Poldervaart, structurally my office-manager and transcriber. She has filled the structural rôles admirably, faithfully typing and processing the hand-written text and patiently copying revisions. But far beyond supplying the technical infra-structure, Marianne has understood my personal instructions and called me back to them when I wavered. She is spiritual mentor and sister, therapeutic colleague, student and teacher of healing energy, and friend through thick and thin. Marianne has been a nurturant container for the book and its scribe.

Thank you people.

Robert D. Phillips
Chapel Hill, N.C.
April 1995

Dedication

To my children, in order of appearance
   My one son: Bo
   My six daughters: Stuart
         Helen
         Jane
         Anna
         Betsy
         Fran

And to the Duke University residents in psychiatry during the past twenty-two years.

To all of them, and to my patients. These human animals, the bright and the brave, have been my students, my teachers, and my blessings.

Chapter 1

The Human Animal

WEARING A THREE-PIECE SUIT, A FASHIONABLE dress, football gear, a military uniform, work clothes or even a bikini, the people we see in our fields of vision and in our mirrors bear little resemblance to the other living species.

Locomotion by feet and wings and dorsal fins has been usurped by wheels and engines and sails, all effectively separating humankind from the other animals and from much of the natural world.

As we glance at the crowds hurrying through the market-place we might conclude that most of them are efficient and purposeful, that their lives confer satisfaction and meaning.

However closer observation and close-in listening to individuals in the crowd would tend to support Thoreau's somber contention that "the mass of men lead lives of quiet desperation." [1]

Behind the smiling determined facades and removed from electronic buzz and whirr, we discover that modern men and women are anxious, depressed, worried, restless, and unfulfilled. Beyond some indisputable benefits from its labor-saving and life-saving machinery, industrialization has robbed us of our connectedness with nature, with the other animals, and frequently with our own souls. We have become alienated from our animalness; we have suppressed it, denied it, sanitized it, or renounced it. I am persuaded that, in order to recover our full humanity, it is necessary to recover our animalness.

This book is a sympathetic and sober description and a celebrative story about the "human animal." In referring to us and our kind I'll mainly use that term, which emphasizes our biology. There are useful and familiar synonyms — human, human being, people, and person. "Man" is neither useful nor acceptable in its implied exclusion of "woman." The effort to be politically correct by using the form he/she or she/he, or by alternating the feminine and masculine references to encompass the species is awkward and a weak remedy for established grammatical sexism.

The term "human animal" will recur repeatedly throughout the book in a pattern designed to re-orient us to our original and natural heritage. For relief from a drumbeat repetition, the terms "people" and "person" will be used also. In an increasingly depersonalized society the word "person" has a corrective thrust, in spite of its shady derivation from the Latin root, *persona*, which means "a mask."

Although other species are adept at camouflage it is only the human animal who devises masks, concrete and metaphorical. The use of disguise and pretense allows us to live lives of falsehood, and that unsavory capacity undergirds a major portion of this human chronicle — the construction of what I call the False Self System. The writer of Ecclesiastes foreshadowed my clinical observations with this wry comment: "I have found that God, when he made man, made him straightforward, but man invents endless subtleties of his own."

The subtitle phrase "In and Out of Therapy" has several implications which need explication. First, "therapy" is used as a generic term signifying "healing power." Psychotherapy is only one of the myriad of specific therapies which are applied from outside the sufferer. The most important "healing powers" are those which are inside the sufferer, inherent to the human animal. Foremost among those are the processes of wound-healing and the activities of the immune system.

I am a psychiatrist and I believe that it behooves us to expect cycles of being "in and out of psychotherapy" throughout life. The inevitable occurrences of wounding and the natural responses of healing guarantee that we will be in and out of restorative therapy, whether or not we engage a designated "healer."

In this book I intend to share beliefs about the "natural history" of the human animal and observations about the un-natural distortions of that history. From scientific observation we can draw for all the other species a clear and reliably predictable picture of species-specific natural histories. Not so with the human species, possessed as it is with "free-will" which affords a vast repertoire of responses and options not bound by evolution or instinct. But it is part of our distorted false-self history that we typically overestimate the freedom-of-choice permitted by freewill. The facts are that we are still very much bound by instinctual response and that we are profoundly influenced by our "herd."

Even more we are bound and limited by the "unfinished business" of our childhoods. That "business" includes unrequited love, odious favoritism, overt and subtle abuse, untrue diminutions and false elevations, misinformation, overprotection, inadequate protection, insufficient nurture, and emotional extortion. Those woundings occur in the family-of-origin, even in the best of families.

Collectively these woundings are called "unresolved conflicts." They are internalized, incorporated, and largely sealed-off as the unconscious polluted streams which divert and befoul the healthy outflow of our natural histories. It is my belief that those subterranean waters can be purified and reconnected to the healthy reservoir only through that therapy called psychotherapy. And I am fully persuaded that the only psychotherapy which assists that redirection is one which requires of both the patient *and* the therapist that they descend together into the forbidding murky depths.

There are two principal forces or realities which guarantee that the human animal will be wounded early and repetitively. One of those forces, human free will is inside the person; the other, environmental reality, is outside.

Free-will allows human beings to override instinct and therewith to exceed natural healthy limitations. Human grandiosity injures the individual and society by violating natural law and then requiring that someone else pick up the pieces. Also free-will allows people to refuse to "go along with the crowd (herd, tribe, society)." That standing-alone is the template for healthy individuation, but it guarantees the wounds of rejection, loneliness, and isolation.

We are born into the environments of nature and society and each of us has to adapt continually to those variable environments. Some of those environments are toxic and injurious: arsenic and lead, blizzards and solar rays, bacteria and viruses, parasites and predators, poverty and oppression, vehicles and verbiage, exploitation and betrayal, falsehood and pretense. Other elements are healing and restorative: oxygen and lithium, rain and breeze, aloe and digitalis, molds and minerals, pets and mounts, charity and liberation, tools and literature, intimacy and reconciliation, truthfulness and realism. Throughout life the human participates constantly and simultaneously lives in both environments, the wounding one and the healing one. The natural state of health is not one of invulnerability nor of permanent cure, but one in which the human animal experiences perpetual cycles of predictable injury and reliable recovery.

It is reassuring to remember that recovery (healing) always follows injury (wounding), until the last moment of life. And it is morale-boosting to realize that recovery is always far more than a return to "the pre-morbid condition" (a morbid medical term meaning, "the way things used to be"). The process of recovery for the human animal is always *growth-producing*, not just an arithmetic return to zero.

For the other animal species it is apparently true that recovery does mean only the return to a prior state of healthy functioning. But for the human animal who is so grievously wounded in childhood, *every* later sequence of wounding and healing recovers something of the sufferer's original purity of health. Returning to my earlier image of effective psychotherapy involving a descent into the depths, I can now talk about recovery in the metaphor of retrieving "hidden treasure," from underneath the pools of the unconscious. That treasure consists of all those natural talents, capacities, creative energies, and autonomous dreams which were denied, discouraged, disallowed, or threatened by exploitative takeover in the family-of-origin. Every child hid those treasures and for safety's sake threw away the key. It is the privilege and task of the psychotherapist to work in concert with the patient (sufferer) to mint a new key, unique in its notches and grooves which only the patient can identify.

To illustrate the concept of recovery as "growth beyond healing," one can look to the realms of perspective and attitude. As children we are taught: "The doctor cures us"; and "Parents know best." Such teachings promote an infantile dependence on authority and an attitude of inadequacy within the child. Grandiosity is "in the air" in such an imbalance, generally imputed to the authority, but secretly incubated by the child as well. In later life we have repeated opportunity, with each cycle of wounding and healing, to regain perspective and to revise attitude. In the healthy state of adult *interdependence*, we gain the perspective that our own healing power is the final authority, to which doctors and parents are supportive consultants. And we exchange the attitude of grandiosity for that of humble gratitude.

I am drawing word-pictures of the human animal, of the species' natural history, of the distortions of that history, and of the special therapies needed for the variety of woundings.

In addition to the woundings from family life, from free-will, from social adaptation, and from injurious nature there is yet another prominent source of unhealth. That is the belief-system of each particular culture, conveying as it does pervasive dogmas and doctrines which are not true. Such beliefs are usually self-serving for the cultural leaders and are generally discriminatory against the "outsiders."

Two cultures which have powerfully affected my perspective and my life stand in sharp contrast with each other. I quote representative spokespersons for each of them:

David, the Jewish shepherd-warrior named King by the patriarchy, asks a rhetorical question as to the nature of human beings. Addressing Jehovah *he* inquires: "What is man that you should be mindful of him; the son of man that you should seek him out?"

Disarmingly lyrical, the slingshooting harpist answers his own question in royalist and sexist language:

"You have made him but little lower than the angels;
You adorn him with glory and honor.
You give him mastery over the works of your hands;
You put all things under his feet:
All sheep and oxen, even the wild beasts of the field,
The birds of the air, the fish of the sea, and whatsoever
    walks in the paths of the sea." [2]

(from Psalm 8, New Revised Standard Version)

The Judeo-Christian anthropology which David faithfully represents becomes the presumptive (and presumptuous) anthropology of the Western world. "Man," especially male-man, emerges as the earthly lord, having dominion over a creation at his disposal.

Oren Lyons, the contemporary Iroquois orator became a chief through ordination of the Haudenosaunee clan mothers. His perspective contrasts sharply with David's and he well represents the assumptions of America's indigenous people. In an address to the Non-Governmental Organizations of the United Nations in Geneva, Switzerland, in 1977, Lyons says:

"I do not see a delegation for the Four-footed,
I see no seat for the Eagles.
We forget and we consider ourselves superior.
But we are after all a mere part of Creation.

And we must consider to understand where we are.

And we stand somewhere between the Mountain and the Ant.

Somewhere, and only there as part and parcel of the Creation." [3]

Elsewhere Lyons, the Faithkeeper of the Turtle Clan of the Onondaga Nation, writes:

"Man sometimes thinks he has been elevated to be the controller, the ruler. But he's not. He's only a part of the whole. Man's job is not to exploit but to oversee, to be a steward. Man has responsibility, not power."

"In our way of life, in our government, with every decision we make, we always keep in mind the Seventh Generation to come. It's our job to see that the people coming ahead, the generations still unborn, have a world no worse than ours — and hopefully better. When we walk upon Mother Earth we always plant our feet carefully because we know the faces of our future generations are looking up at us from beneath the ground. We never forget them."

Those understandings of the human being as having dominion over nature (e.g., the Judeo-Christian) not only encourage people to exploit the environment but they also render people oblivious to the powerful effects of the environment on them.

The model of the human animal which I propose can be understood only as that animal is seen in dynamic relationship with its multiple concentric environments. Health or unhealth of the individual animal apart from the environment is a myth.

In a culture which is doggedly individualistic and devoted to measurement, the crucial factors of balance and harmony with the environments are replaced by concerns about "normal values." But health depends not so much on the right numbers (blood pressure, cholesterol, calcium, weight, or aerobic capacity) as on the "right" relationship with the environment. Whether the environment of the moment is mainly another person or a segment of nature or society the "right" relationship can only be one which is reciprocally enriching and growthful. So in my models of health, unhealth, healing and therapy I orient around the recovery and maintenance of natural balance, harmony, and rhythm.

As psychotherapist I too am one of the environmental elements or objects to which my patients are exposed. It is my responsibility, invoking Oren Lyons' perspective, to avoid exploitation of the people I work with, but rather to oversee and to be a good steward. I have responsibility. I do not have power to fix or change or cure other human beings, unilaterally. I cannot help another by *imposing* my will or my wisdom or even my loving concern upon that other. I can and I do help when that other and I enter a consultative partnership within which we exchange information and energy and caring.

The therapist, and perhaps the psychotherapist especially, must recognize creaturely kinship with those people who come for healing; The therapist is not the controller or the ruler, but the *attendant*. One of the definitions of therapy is "healing power," and my preferred understanding of the therapist's function is that of attending. Attending means listening; it means sitting-with; it means learning-with; it means attuning-to; and it means subordinating to the leadership of the patient's own healing power.

"Attending" may sound like inaction, and subordination may sound like passive deferment. In point of fact attentive psychotherapists listen openly but they simultaneously filter the incoming information through their theoretical constructions and through belief-systems about human function and behavior. If one is alert one always hears something novel in the familiar and something of precedent in all new information. Neither attendance nor preparation for attendance is passive or vague. The attending psychotherapist can remain quiet, subordinate, and therefore helpful only if he or she has confidence in his or her theoretical model and confidence in the healing power of the patient.

(You will notice that I am using the term "patient" to designate the person who seeks healing. Recent downturning developments in Western society have rendered that time-honored word politically suspect if not politically-incorrect.

Until the recent past decades the "doctor-patient" relationship was held in semi-sacred trust. Combinations of physician-greed, fragmenting specialization, distancing hands-off technology, and the adversarial threat of malpractice suits have combined to erode that trust.

Presumptions of special privilege and the exploitation of dependents have been increasingly challenged, and hitherto acceptable terms like "housewife," "common laborer," "unskilled worker," "servant" have been subjected to political correction. Similarly with the term "patient." And in the field of psychotherapy especially there has been objection on the part of non-medical practitioners to a label which comes from the "medical model." The term "client" fits a relationship which might be less intimate but also less exploitable; "client" is synonymous with "customer" or "patron."

I want to preserve the word "patient" and to restore it to its original connotation of "sufferer" or "wounded one" or "one-in-pain." It is the patient's suffering that should be the starting place in the healing relationship and it should be the continual touchstone. It might be useful to shift the emphasis by referring to the "patient-attendant" relationship.)

My emphasis on the environment requires some special terminology which will be introduced piecemeal in the text. Perhaps the most important "new" word is *container*. The idea of the holding, cuddling, nutrient environment is so dear and familiar to me that I have been surprised to learn that the word "container" does not evoke that picture for many people. Obviously (perhaps not so obviously in an individualistic society) the idea of the containing environment is a derivative extension of the infant's experience of being held healthfully by the mothering person.

I discovered (or was discovered by) the viable Native American culture five years ago. I felt relieved and confirmed to find an entire people with ancient and continuing lineage who take as their major reality a reciprocal relationship with "Mother Earth," indeed with mothering creation. For the indigenous people of North America, the *circle* is far more than a symbol; it is the embodied template for containing and being contained.

It is true that my therapeutic life and my personal life have been considerably influenced and substantially confirmed through my association with Native Americans. I believe that my acquaintance with Oren Lyons (Onondaga) and Janine Windy Boy (Crow) and Tom Porter (Mohawk), and Roberta Blackgoat (Dine-Navajo), and Lloyd Owle (Cherokee) and Sequoyah Trueblood (Choctaw), and Marilyn Pourier (Lakota Sioux) and with the ways of their people has hastened my recovery, a recovery of perspective and initiative, of what my native friends would call "remembering my instructions."

Apropos of those instructions, I am comforted to recall Robert Frost's lines from *Into My Own:*

"They would not find me changed from him they knew:
Only more sure of what he always knew was true." [4]

Birth into society guarantees loss of initiative. The collective units of society, from family to institutions, tell us what to do and it is mainly in our best interest to "do it."

Participation in the culture guarantees loss of perspective. The builders of culture, from the individual artist to the institutions of church and state, overwhelm us with stimulation and with the temptation to idolize. Culture obscures our view of nature, that immediate expression of Mother Earth, which restores perspective and balance.

Psychotherapy helps the human animal recover animalness while continuing to participate in society and culture. But psychotherapy has a particular mission of expertise which is not addressed by other remedies and which cannot be accomplished by the "natural healings" of time or of love.

The human animal is wounded by the injudicious exercise of free will. And the human animal is bound still by instinct, by genetic variance, and by the random viccisitudes of life. But again the particular binding addressed by psychotherapy is that which issues from the unresolved conflicts of early family life. Those conflicts are incorporated closed-system operations which will be repetitively and unconsciously acted on and acted out until they are opened up and exposed to the light of day and to the light of communal acceptance.

There are recurrent woundings from society, and culture, and from "acts of God"; and there is a "fixed" unhealth incorporated from childhood. Each psychotherapeutic intervention can assist the patient in only a partial detoxification of that "fixed" unhealth, of the unresolved conflicts. After each intervention, the force and influence of the "unfinished business" is reduced and the stream of unconscious conflict returns to the depths. It will come to consciousness again another day, roused by some associated life-event, by dreams, or meditation, or by the deliberate homework of psychotherapy. Its return is the next opportunity for further recovery.

In this first chapter I have shared some beliefs about the human animal and about the nature of psychotherapy.

In subsequent chapters I'll flesh-out the description of the human animal and I'll illustrate the psychotherapeutic process by telling real stories about fictitious people.

I present a radically simple model of the Person (the human animal) which will require some attentive study on your part. The concepts of the two parts of the Person, which are the Ego and the Self, will be seen as different from some traditional models.

My particular training will be reflected in my theories and constructions. I was trained initially in psychoanalytic psychotherapy. Later I studied Gestalt therapy and psychodrama and Transactional Analysis. I learned General Systems Theory Therapy and I read from the Existential therapists.

Some of the later teachers who especially influenced my thinking were Melanie Klein and Donald W. Winnicott of the British, psychoanalytic community. Winnicott wrote extensively about the "maternal holding environment," the literal precursor to the concept of "the container."

In this book I expose and emphasize the extent of the wounding that falls to every human animal. I talk about the inexorable nature of the False Self System's takeover, about the inevitability of some degree of surrender to oppression, and I talk about the indomitable insistence of the True Self on liberation, recovery, and growth.

The True Self is like that solitary blade of grass which somehow pushes itself upward through the thickness of a concrete walkway.

On her valedictory visit one of my patients left a grateful poem she had written honoring our work together. The punch-line was:

"Even Freud was right, old botanist:
He said green things grow together toward the light."

Chapter 2

Tom's Dream: Tom's Drama

TOM CAME TO SEE ME EIGHTEEN MONTHS AGO WANTING TO change a pattern of recurrent "failures" in romantic relationships. He is currently dating a woman some twenty years his junior — he identifies his attraction to glamorous younger women as part of the pattern.

At a recent session Tom reported a vivid dream which occurred after a telephone conversation with his woman-friend Carol just at bedtime. Tom and Carol regularly end the day with a telephoned goodnight when they aren't sleeping together. On this occasion Carol had sounded weary and discouraged by the stresses of her work; she's a school counselor. Tom recognized and restrained his impulse to suggest to Carol that he drive the several miles to her home and "tuck her in." Tom is also a psychotherapist and with his head he knows better than to leap to someone's unsolicited rescue, especially that of a damsel-in-distress. He told Carol that she sounded stressed; in a more energetic voice she denied that she was. He wished her a good night's sleep and said good-bye. Tom said to me, "I turned out the light and thought for a while. I was pleased with myself for not falling into my rescue-trap, but I noticed that I was anxious as hell. I went on off to sleep and had this dream."

"It's one of those dreams where I'm one of the characters but I'm also watching the dream. Anyway in the opening scene there's some kind of small transparent house — actually just one room with glass everywhere — sitting in a field surrounded by a tremendous crowd of people packed all the way to the horizon. I was inside the room with twenty-nine other people; somehow I knew there were exactly thirty of us. From up above where I was watching the dream it seemed for sure that the little glass room would be squashed by the huge crowd. Inside the room I felt some anxiety but really more curiosity. Whatever this was seemed awfully important but mainly bizarre. I didn't actually recognize any of the other twenty-nine in the room, but I knew that they were 'my' people — whatever that meant. When I had first looked out at the crowd they seemed basically friendly, but they really weren't paying much attention to us. When I looked again they were all staring at us and smiling, but their smiles were not friendly — you know, those smiles that say I know something you don't know. And then it was obvious that they were pressing in on us, not hard but steady. Then I did get anxious. I asked out loud, 'Are we the good ones?' From behind me someone answered, 'You know we are the good ones!' It was a man's voice, deep and reassuring and kinda amused or indulgent or something like that. I felt safer for a moment, until I looked out again at the mass of people. This time their faces looked really mean. Then I asked, pointing to the crowd, 'Well, who are they?' The deep voice spoke again, 'They are the good hyphen evil people, the most hurtful of all.'"

Tom said that when he awakened from the dream around dawn he first felt the aftermath anxiety. But then he noticed some excitement of discovery and a sense that this dream was a great gift; that it contained "all the stuff that I came into therapy to work on."

In dream-work I start with the assumption that every single element in a dream — all the people, all the buildings, all the spaces, all the objects, all the attitudes of all the players — represents a projected "piece" of the dreamer. There seem always to be universal themes and symbols in dreams, but there are also themes and unfoldings which are unique to the dreamer. The unique themes in Tom's current life were conditioned by the particular circumstances of early life in his family of origin. Those themes recur not only in his dream-life but in his personal relationships and work life as well.

Tom was the second of two sons born to parents who were manifestly "good people." They were peaceful and peace-making people who didn't overtly display "negative" feelings toward each other, inside or outside the home. They were productive, sociable, religious, charitable, loyal, reliable, uncomplaining, witty, politically concerned, and family-oriented. They were attentive to their children, their adult siblings and their parents — attentive across three generations. Chores assigned to the sons were traditional, regular and reasonable. The necessity and benefit of corporal punishment for misbehavior was assumed and it was mercifully unaccompanied by lectures or editorials. The parents and the large extended family practiced and preached the noble obligation of taking care of those in less-fortunate circumstance. The family taught its members to count blessings instead of hurts or deprivations or disappointments. High value was placed on cheerfulness and on the stiff-upper-lip in adversity. The picture of a secure, stable and loving family emerged as Tom talked about his childhood. In painting the broad strokes of his family portrait, Tom seemed to express surprise as well as pride when he said, "I really did have a happy childhood."

From earliest recall, Tom told me, it seemed clear that his mother favored his older brother. He added, rather matter-of-factly, that by the time he started school he had "heard" that he was his father's favorite and he thought then and now that was true.

It was frequently reported in Tom's hearing that he had "always been a good baby — that he was just born with a good disposition." In the sessions with me he recalled that he once took pride in that acknowledgment — but now he mainly felt sadness about it. He had learned in his therapy training that "good children" are frequently those who were not allowed natural fretting and yelling in infancy because of parental needs. Tom remembered an oft-told story about his "cute" little boy self being frightened by a thunderstorm and saying to his parents, "I wouldn't be scared if I just knew I was a good boy." Currently Tom believes, and I concur, that he learned an obligatory "goodness" and then parlayed that requirement into a repertoire of "good" behaviors calculated to impress his mother. Tom was genuinely grateful for the close relationship with his father ("We were real buddies."), but he recognized that he had always been driven to win his mother's approval and hopefully her preference.

The mother's only ostentation was her moralistic piety, based on a variety of Thou-shalt-nots. Foremost among the contraband taboos were alcohol, tobacco, irreverence, disobedience, vainglory, sex, and aggression. All violations were punishable by silence. When Tom's mother was morally offended by her husband or her sons she gave them the "silent treatment." Tom reported that with some hardness in his voice. He recalled a mixture of feelings — anger, pity, embarrassment, compassion, and anxiety — welling up whenever he saw his father "following Mother around the house, trying to get her to say something when she was in that hard cold place."

Sarah, the unrelenting judge, was also the witty and affectionate woman who lovingly devoted her life to caring for her husband and her sons. She was a traditional Southern woman, trained to feed in the Southern way, which is in itself an oral tradition. (The mouth and its functions are so highly valued throughout the Bible Belt in part because other organs are so little valued, especially the apparatuses of elimination and procreation.)

Sarah was a skilled and tender feeder, a cornucopia of foodstuffs, social graces, good literature, high principles, homilies, family anecdotes, word-play, proverbs, quotations from the Bible and the classics, and ministrations to wounds her men received *outside* the home. From Sarah's kitchen came three hot meals a day — generous portions of simple nutritious fare, loaded with cholesterol, love, calories, pleasure, salt, familiarity, sweets, and kindness. Tom told me that he thought his older brother John had needed to defend himself against excessive attention from their mother. So John was the only one in the family who was not overweight. He was serious, skinny, and somewhat aloof; Tom and his parents were fat and jolly. Sarah ate just enough of her own cooking to neutralize all sensuous contour but not enough to detract from her very pretty face.

Every infant's primary caregiving female becomes the model and symbol of Woman. That model can be copied, modified, reversed or rejected but its imprint is forever. During childhood Tom devoted much of his life's energy to changing himself to please Sarah or to getting Sarah to change for his benefit. Neither of those projects was successfully con-summated, so Tom has repeated his reflex repertoire over and over in romantic relationships. The fossil remains of Sarah's influence would be hard to recognize in most of Tom's chosen wives and lovers, but the common threads are there and Tom is increasingly able to identify them.

If Tom never succeeded in becoming his mother's Chosen One, he experienced several rapturous approximations, sufficient to fire his hope and expectancy for life. His later courtship style has been characterized by ardor, daring, persistence, and optimism. Reviewing these patterns one day, he reported rather matter-of-factly, "The women I have gotten involved with thought I was wonderful at first and they said so." Tom fell silent. As if listening to a faint sound, he looked uncertain and then startled. "My God, I remember Mother saying that to me a few times and I thought the kingdom had come!" His rapid breathing and flushed face reflected Tom's excitement as he reported the memory of glory from age four.

Tom said, "I don't know why I said four but that seems right. Anyway I went into the kitchen when Mother was cooking. Nobody else was home. She had just been talking on the phone and she was sitting in a chair crying without making any noise — that's the only way she ever cried. She didn't look up so I started to leave, but I didn't. I went over and patted her and said, "I love you." She looked up and just smiled a little bit and then she hugged me and said, "You're my wonderful little man. I couldn't get along without you."

Slowly Tom returned to the present with me. His eyes were watery but clear. "Damn! Do you think I really remember that or did I make it up or what?" I smiled. Tom laughed and added, "I know what you're thinking — that the facts don't matter. Is that right? Yeah, that's right. Whether I made it up or not I've been looking for a repeat of that all my life, haven't I?"

Yes.

Chapter 3

FREE WILL AND THE SCRIPT

IT APPEARS THAT ALL OF THE ANIMALS OTHER THAN THE HUMAN animal have an uncomplicated family-life. "Child-rearing" among those animals looks rather simple and straightforward. The offspring are born, they are faithfully fed and fiercely protected for a while, then they are sent out into the world, apparently without sentiment or strings attached.

Presumably the other animals are limited to instinctual behavior and do not possess "free-will" — a blessing and a curse reserved to the human animal.

People are biological animals also and each one arrives with a built-in genetically-coded instinctual program. Free-will allows the human animal to follow the instinctual program, or to modify it, or even to defy it. Animals without free-will respond to a variety of *needs* which arise rhythmically and periodically during the days and months and seasons. Among those needs are food and shelter and mating and procreation and migration.

Human animals have all those instinctual needs, but they also have wills and wants and wishes. Desire can supplement, modify, replace, or symbolically substitute for natural biological need. Human desire (will) is a blessing when it allows the human animal to transcend instinctual need for some "higher goal" or to increase options. It is a curse when it allows the animal to convert repetitive desire into habituated craving and then into fixed addiction. Free-will is a blessing when it allows a parent to suspend the need for food or sleep in order to tend to a wounded frightened child. It is a curse when it allows human beings, especially parents, to intrude their own wills-wishes-wants into other human beings, especially into children.

Tom's free-will and his instinctual responsiveness had both been reduced by the weight of the "family will," especially by the dominant will of his mother. Her vision for him replaced his vision for himself. In these consequences Tom is typical of socialized human animals, particularly of those raised in "mainly-good" families.

Transactional Analysis, the theoretical model of human interaction developed by Eric Berne, has made a number of useful contributions to the science of human behavior. Among those is the concept of the "script," an essentially unconscious program intruded into the developing child by family messages and models. The "script" is an unhealthy program consisting of parental messages which run counter to the child's natural ground-plan and of parental models which demonstrate un-natural self-effacement or self-inflation. The child must accept the "script" because acceptance is a precondition of being cared for by the family. That requirement applies particularly to emotional caring, in the conveyances of affection and approval and "love."

Ideally family life for the human animal would more nearly resemble that of the other animals. In the best-case scenario parents would tend their young by supplying food and information and companionship and comfort when the *child* asks for those things. The child's emerging needs and wishes would not dominate but they would regularly take priority over parental convenience or whim. Ideally the parents would always resist the temptation to exploit the child's appearance or performance for their own glory or for their own self-pitying shame.

A contemporary bumper-sticker boasts, "Proud parent of a terrific kid." Perhaps that claim is made by parents who want it known that they are not indifferent or neglectful. It sounds good, but the claim is hazardous. Lodged in this good-sounding slogan are elements of ownership and implications of conditionality ("I love my child because she's terrific; I won't love my child if she's not"). And at it's subtle worst the prideful claim suggests that the parent is taking personal credit for the child's blossoming.

Human parents impose and intrude the "script program" in large part because they do not trust the child's inborn program. In short they do not trust nature. The non-human species and the indigenous humans who live intimately with the natural world maintain a detached expectancy about their offsprings' futures. But the dominant Western society subdues Nature and exploits her riches for self-aggrandizement and material gain. Successive generations in the Christianized industrialized West have been persuaded that salvation, healing, repair, wisdom, direction and fulfillment all come from *outside* the individual.

Ideally parents would trust their own intuition as well as the child's inherent competence and sturdiness. In that circle of trust, the child would be encircled by a love that was constant but flexible. Sometimes the child would be held tightly, sometimes the child would be allowed free-roaming space, but whether near or far, the initiation would be with the child. The parents would not conceive of the child's behaviors in terms of "good" or "bad" so much as "useful" or "not useful." And they would *never* label the child "good" or "bad." Social skills would be taught as necessary adaptations for living in community; they would not be used as merit-points for parental approval or glorification. And social skills would not be allowed to substitute for the nurtured qualities of thoughtfulness, kindness, consideration, sensitivity, and empathy.

In simple terms the "script" is a program of messages which tell the child to be things she isn't (e.g. Be Perfect) and to not be things she is (e.g. Don't Be Emotional). Well-meaning parents who don't examine their own parenting behaviors are left to repeat the mistakes of their own family history, unwittingly doing unto their children what was done unto them. And anxious mistrust of the human interior leaves the parent susceptible to a variety of ancient competitions, compensations, vicarious substitutions, and discounts from the generational family of origin — all again to be visited unconsciously on the children of today.

Mistrust of the other person's natural inclination toward health and growth spawns a readiness to critique, correct, and control. And those behaviors do indeed promote untrustworthiness and mistrust in the other (child or spouse or colleague); so the vicious circle of mistrust is established.

Chapter 4

A CELLULAR MODEL AND THE FALSE SELF SYSTEM

THERE IS A LOT OF TALK THESE DAYS ABOUT THE SELF AS A part of the human personality. Neither the scientific community (psychology and anthropology) nor the academic community (theology and the humanities) has brought much clarity or agreement to the concept of the Self.

At this point I need to provisionally define the terms, *True Self* and *False Self*, the first term being required only because of the existence of the second. The "True Self" is not exactly synonymous with "the Soul," but for now let us agree that they are the same. And the "False Self" is not precisely the ghost-writing author of the "script" but that connection will do for now.

The human animal makes models in order to make meaning of the past and present and to plan ahead for the future. Model-making and model-following are such characteristic human behaviors that we don't notice how extraordinary they actually are, given the here-and-now realism of the rest of Nature. Model-making is yet another gift and burden of free-will. As gift it allows a vision of what one can become; as burden it imposes a picture of what one "ought to" be. Gifted model-making takes the form of "positive imaging" and it enhances realization of the True Self. Burdensome model-making focuses on flaws, deficits, and imperfections and as such provides the template for the False Self system.

More will follow about model-making, but at this point I'll share some verbal and visual models of True Self and False Self. And in order to do that I have to enlist an associated vocabulary which includes yet some more abstract terms; these are *ego, narcissism, object-relating,* and *environment.* I use these terms in very particular ways in constructing my model of the human animal. You will find this model and its vocabulary to be different from some traditional models, but quite familiar in other respects.

My picture of the human animal can best be understood as a *cellular model.* The living biological cell is the smallest, most basic circumscribed unit in the body. It makes useful sense to me to conceive of the human body and indeed the human person as being a magnified representation of the single cell.

Following are visual and verbal models of (Fig 1) the biological cell and, in extension, (Fig 2) of the human animal, and then of the transposed (Fig 3) cellular model and finally of (Fig 4) the False Self System.

(Fig 1) *The Biological Cell*   Environment
(Cells and Fluid)

Environment
(Cells and Fluid)

Cell Membrane

Environment
(Cells and Fluid)

Cell Nucleus

Environment
(Cells and Fluid)

All living matter, all organisms, are made up of cells which have two basic components, a nucleus and an outer membrane. The nucleus contains the instructions for the cell, both its "standing orders" about how to be a particular cell (e.g. skin cell, nerve cell, stomach cell, etc.) and its ad hoc directions for staying in balance under changing conditions. The nucleus is, in effect, the cell's primitive brain. The outer membrane, also called "the limiting membrane," is the circumferential boundary. That membrane is the container for the cell, much as an inflated balloon is container for the air within it. It is also the defining border between the cell and the surrounding environment. Ordinarily the environment (also known as the "surround," the "field," or "the outside world") consists of adjacent cells which, like the subject cell, are suspended in fluid of a particular electrochemical activity. The cell membrane is semi-permeable; that is, it has windows which can be opened or shut to allow the commerce of intake and output with the environment. The principal ad hoc function of the nucleus is to signal the membrane to open or close selectively in order to maintain a "steady-state" balance with the outside.

(Fig 2) *The Human Animal* (The Person)

Environment
(Society and Nature)

THE EGO
(The Object-Relating Organ)

Environment
(Society and Nature)

Environment
(Society and Nature)

THE SELF
(The Narcissistic Organ)

Environment
(Society and Nature)

The human animal is born into the world with two destinies, one object-relatedness and the other self-fulfillment. These destinies are expressed through two basic organs or agents, the Ego and the Self.

In my model the Ego refers to everything about the Person, body and mind, which relates that person to the surrounding environment. That environment consists of Society and Nature. The Ego is everything about the Person except the Self. The Ego includes the entire physical body, the developed brain and nervous system, all the senses, the sensations and the emotions, beliefs and perspectives, the electrochemical energy, the neurohormonal energy, and all the energies of interdependent attachment. The Ego and its elements are substantive and they are quantifiable, either by measurement or inference. The business of the Ego is the business of science, of material reality. It operates in observable space and in recordable time; indeed it is the agent of the space-time world.

The Self is non-Ego and therefore cannot be measured or defined. It is spirit and like the wind, its natural counterpart, is invisible but it can be "known" by its effect. The Self has no quantity but it confers quality in the Person. Personal quality is made up of such specific qualities as kindness, determination, patience, self-discipline, toughness, empathy, ambition, creativity, faith, transcendence, idealism, truthfulness, integrity, gratitude, and non-attaching love.

(Fig 3) *The Cellular Model*

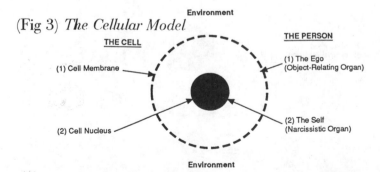

The term, "narcissistic," has been unobtrusively slipped into the model in relation to the Self. Much more about "narcissism" later.

You will have noticed that the cellular model consists of only two explicit parts. This arrangement is distinguished from traditional models of human personality which have three parts or layers; e.g. the psychoanalytic construction of id, ego, and superego, or in another rendering, unconscious, preconscious, and conscious. A derivative model from Transactional Analysis portrays Child, Adult, and Parent Ego-states. It is not coincidental that humans have conceived of a three-storied universe; e.g. Heaven, Earth, Hell.

The cellular model represents the human animal in its original form, at birth. Newly born into the world, before being "sinned" against, the child is integrated, both in its personhood and with the environment. There is no split between Ego and Self and no perceived conflict between Person and Environment. That state of grace and integrity is short-lived however, as Society quickly begins to "sin" against the infant by imposition or neglect. The infant's brief resistance to imposition and brief complaint about neglect are collectively called Original Sin, a crime charged to the victim. In order to survive, the infant-child surrenders initiative to the parental structures (biological parents, surrogates, and experts) and then colludes with them in the construction of the False Self System.

(Fig 4) *The False Self System*

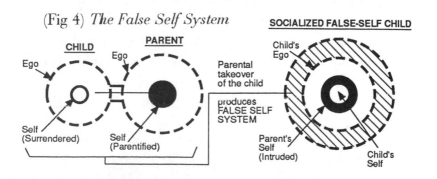

I noted above that the natural cellular model has only two basic elements, nuclear self and containing Ego. And this was in contrast to the traditional three-layered models of the personality and the universe.

However it is obvious that in the False Self System's distortion of the cellular model, there is indeed a third "layer," that of the parental director. And this False Self System model can be seen to make common cause with the psychoanalytic model in which the outside "layer," the superego, is understood as the internalized agent of parents and society.

And now it can be appreciated that in fact the system of the natural cellular model does have an implicit third "layer," which is the harmonious nurturant environment. (The indigenous peoples call that environment by her name, Mother Earth.)

In the contra-natural False Self System the boundaries between Self and Ego and those between Ego and Environment have been unhealthily altered, either too thickened or too thinned out. In response to parenting which is either too rigid (impositional) or too lax (neglectful) such boundaries make for interpersonal isolation or for symbiotic merger. In such a system the relationships between Self and Ego and Environment are characterized by suspicion and alienation rather than by the original attitudes of trust and harmony.

I anticipate the dénouèment of this human predicament when I say that the basic goals of psychotherapy are the dismantling of the False Self System and the recovery and restoration of the True Self System.

And the particular goals of psychotherapy reflect the broader goal of the human life cycle; that is, to unfold and grow while repetitively healing from injury, old and new. Therefore, it is for a lifetime that the human animal is in and out of therapy.

Chapter 5

SANDRA'S REVENGE: SANDRA'S RECOVERY

S ANDRA WAS A GRADUATE STUDENT IN SLAVIC STUDIES WHEN she was referred to me by her faculty advisor for treatment of "dissertation block" and suicidal fantasies.

When she came for her initial interview, there were several things about Sandra that were obvious. She was black, beautiful, mistrustful, and somewhere between proud and arrogant. Her up-East speech was tight and her carefully-crafted sentences were sculpted by her incisors. Her precision and tight control felt ominous to me. The "child" inside my therapist-self wondered, "Does she bite?"

Sandra recounted her symptom-story of two months' duration in an almost journalistic style, as if reading from someone else's life. She was two-thirds finished with her dissertation and thought that she was over the hump. But she awakened one morning after fitful sleep and disturbing dreams and felt immobilized. From that day until she came to see me she had not written a word, although she "put" herself at her desk several times a day. Whenever she looked at the last entered paragraphs on her word-processor screen she would see instead "movies" of her self-inflicted death. She "projected" (her word) an unending series of films, none of which carried much feeling and none which seemed "just right." With a wry smile like William Buckley's, Sandra reported that she amused herself with the idea of "Sandra's Suicide I," "Sandra's Suicide II," and so on. She reported with no levity, that many of her suicide scenarios included one or more homicides as well. Several times she imagined mass killings, but when in her mind's eye she "read" the headlines it all seemed so stereotyped and tacky that she then felt foolish. Sandra gave no clinical evidence of being either suicidal or homicidal, but clearly she was tormented by the fantasies' obsessional residence in her thoughts.

I asked Sandra what she wanted to do in therapy. She answered sharply, "I'll tell you exactly what I want to do. I want to get over this block and get on with my career. I want to stop seducing married white men just to mess them up. And I want to get married and have a family."

Sandra was the youngest of three daughters born into modest circumstance in a small Connecticut resort town where there were few black families. Her mother had inherited a small amount of money and a large amount of pride from her people who had lived for at least five generations in the Northeast. The first known Quentin ancestor was a cabinet-maker who had bought his freedom and married a woman who was part-Negro and part-Seneca. Sandra's father was from the South, having moved from Alabama with his employer's family when he was eighteen years old. He was presently, at age fifty-eight, working for that same family as "their man Friday." Sandra's lips tightened around that phrase.

Sandra was not only bright and beautiful. She was also a fine athlete and she said that in school she could hold her own with any of the boys in baseball and basketball. Her parents were very religious. They preached "Christian forgiveness of white people" and "saving sex for marriage."

When Sandra was fourteen, the young white shortstop on the high school baseball team declared his love for her. She resisted his overtures for several months but she felt excitedly in love with him too so they began to date. It was not until six months later that they had sexual intercourse, just three weeks before Hank was leaving for a summer in Europe with his wealthy parents. With more sadness than bitterness Sandra said to me, "I gave him my virginity and after he came back from Europe he never called me again. Later on he married a "rich dumb blonde."

Following her jilting, Sandra said, she was deeply depressed and suicidal. She talked to no one about her wound except her older sister whom she swore to secrecy. Sandra added in a flat mechanical voice that she "recovered without any help" in a few months. She became something of a recluse and a driven scholar. Valedictorian of her class, Sandra received an academic scholarship to Smith where she performed brilliantly in the classroom and vengefully in bed. She had begun her career of seducing married white men.

Sandra's first year in psychotherapy was stormy. As she began relating to me more as person than as captive audience, her thinly-veiled hostility became unveiled. I am male and I am white; Sandra had been abused by both categories and emotionally she expected more of the same. Anticipating attack, she made pre-emptive strikes. She mimicked my Southern accent, and she wondered aloud about racial attitudes of my Dutch South African office-manager. One day she asked more with hostility than with seductiveness, "Have you ever slept with a black woman?"

Between her testings, Sandra worked hard and painfully in psychotherapy. As she and I both survived her angry attacks, she began to write again, haltingly at first. She asked with re-assuring humor, "Will I have to actually hit you to get un-stuck all the way?"

After six months of weekly individual sessions, I persuaded Sandra to join one of my psychotherapy groups. Initially she dismissed my suggestion about group with the rhetorical question, "They'll all be white and middle-class, won't they?"

In the group, indeed all-white and middle-class, Sandra quickly paired with an older woman Millie who was the group's moral watchdog. Millie affectionately hovered but she also silently monitored Sandra, stiffening on those occasions when black anger withered any ingratiating male overture. During her fourth month in the group, Sandra turned angrily one day on the startled Millie, confronting her, "nosey checking-up on people." Before Millie and the others had recovered their practiced composure, Sandra began to cry softly. She looked over at me and said, "I need an individual session with you." The group members were respectful or intimidated or both; no one spoke through Sandra's silence. Someone "changed the subject" as if the confrontation had not occurred.

In individual session several days later, Sandra began calmly. "I had an important insight after I confronted Millie. It shook me up and I just didn't feel like I could deal with it in the group that day. What it had to do with was . . . ." Her voice trailed off and then returned as a strange hoarse cry, deep and feline. She burst into sobs which wracked her dignified and graceful body, returning it to a flailing little-girlness. When she could talk again her verbal precision has gone. She spoke from her broken heart. "I realized the other day that Millie reminded me so much of a bad part of my mother. Mother used to grill me after every date. Sometimes she would examine my underwear. I was guilty until proven innocent. I hated it and I hated her." Sandra paused as her anger dissolved into profound sadness. She looked up at me suspiciously, pitifully. "And guess what," rhetorical and forlorn. "One day I walked in on Mother and the boss's son in bed!" She dropped her head, looking defeated. Finally she looked up, straight into my eyes. "Do you believe me?"

Yes, Sandra, I believe you.

In the next group session Sandra shared her story of shame with her white middle-class friends. She also reported her association between her mother and Millie. All this was met with some tears from men and women, some expressions of advocate outrage, much comforting, and testaments of appreciation for Sandra's courage.

Sandra didn't need to hit me in order to get free, but she apparently did need to uncover the betrayal by her "good parent." She continued in the group for a few months after she was awarded her Ph.D. She had gradually formed a solid supportive network outside the group. It consisted mainly of black women her age. During the year after termination she married a colleague, a highly-regarded Jamaican teaching in Canada.

Chapter 6

Notes On Narcissism

IN GREEK MYTHOLOGY NARCISSUS WAS A SINGULARLY beautiful young man, son of the river-god Cephissus and the nymph Leiriope. A prophet told his mother that Narcissus would have a long and happy life provided he never admired his own beauty. But Narcissus did not heed the warning passed to him by his mother. He rejected the loves of the nymph Echo and of the maiden Ameinias in favor of his own reflection in a pool.

According to psychiatric historians it was Havelock Ellis, the British sex-psychologist, who coined the term narcissism for clinical use in 1898. Western culture in general and psychoanalysis in particular soon adopted the word as meaning excessive self-love. In the popular mind narcissism came to be equated with self-centeredness and selfishness, at the expense of concern for others. And until recently the common clinical views were that narcissism represented either a lingering "immaturity" or a defense against intimate relationships.

In the past twenty-five years evolution of psychoanalytic theory has led to a new "psychology of the Self" which understands narcissistic energy (i.e. energy focused in Self-interest) as a perpetually necessary and vital force. Some Self-psychology schools teach the re-integration of narcissism as a corrective against the centuries-old assumption that Self and Society are enemies. What is heard from the "narcissistic" child as "Me! Me.! Me! Mine! Mine! Mine!" in maturity becomes, "This creative offering will be good for me and for my neighbor." The same energy which feeds the grandiose exhibitionism of the uninhibited child fuels healthy ambition, creativity, and social idealism in the adult.

In the French language two pronouns alone distinguish the two elements of personhood. *Moi* refers to the Ego (the coordinating agency), and *Soi* indicates the Self (the narcissistic factor). The pertinent vocabulary in English is more complicated and in some instances contradictory.

Common usage draws only grammatical distinction between the pronouns *me, myself,* and *I.* And the Latin word "Ego" which is the nominative first-person pronoun meaning "I" has been widely misappropriated to refer to *narcissistic* excess, as in, "He has too much ego."

In point of fact however, when narcissistic energy is expressed injuriously into the environment, it is because there is *too little ego* (too thin a limiting membrane) in operation at the moment. It might well have been that, for a period prior to that moment, the ego was operating (under "parental" orders) to restrain narcissistic energy. And if the ego "let's go" under those conditions there appears to be a narcissistic "explosion," but that appearance does not represent "abnormal" narcissism or self-expression.

The healthy Person has a healthy Ego which, like Janus, has two faces, one turned toward the Self and one toward the environment. Child-rearing which promotes healthy values and capacities for the child provides a flexible containing environment, serving that function until the child's Ego can assume it. Ideally the developing Person will acquire an Ego which looks inward toward the Self with delight, and outward, toward the

Environment with vigilance and expectancy. Such an Ego would replicate the attitude and behaviors of a healthy parental container.

It is unlikely that either a river-god or a nymph would seek psychotherapy for a troubled child, but if either Cephissus or Leiriope telephoned to consult me about their son's anti-social and self-destructive behaviors I would say to them: "Your son Narcissus doesn't need to be less narcissistic. He needs to humanize his Ego. If he is willing to join a therapy group and to work hard we will teach him to alternately say Yes and to say No, sometimes to his Self and sometimes to the Environment. We will help him recover the natural functioning of his Ego so that he will be both kind and tough. Incidentally, you two parents, if you're going to support Narcissus getting into therapy, will have to swallow some of your own false pride."

Following is a. clarifying summary of some relationships between Self, narcissism, Ego, object-relatedness, and the environment:

(1) Self (the narcissistic sector) is unchanging. It does not mature and it does not regress. It needs nothing from the environment but reflection.

(2) The Self is spirit, neither time-bound nor space-bound.

(3) The narcissistic Self is amoral. Morality is an office of the Ego.

(4) Narcissistic energy which is not modified by the value-judgments of the Ego is always injurious in the interpersonal environment. Narcissistic energy not balanced by the Ego's object-relating energy injures other people by grandiose exploitation or by oblivious neglect.

(5) Self-esteem is a function of the Ego looking inward, es-
teeming the Self. A person with adequate self-esteem
also esteems the Self in others; that other-directed es-
teem of the Self-portion is called empathy.

(6) The Ego has relationship both with the Self and with
the Environment. The healthy Ego is environment-
friendly, harvesting gratefully and husbanding wisely.
Ego-maturation allows increasingly reciprocal exchange
with the environment, with other people and with natural resources.

(7) The Ego surrounds, contains, and protects the Self. The
Self informs, instructs, and directs the Ego to actualize
the Self's ideal images. The Self creates dreams of ideal
people, places and arrangements but it is the Ego which
will "carry" the Self in search of those images. When the
Ego locates one such ideal, the Self will whisper or
shout, "That's it!"

Chapter 7

Notes On The Ego

IN SIGMUND FREUD'S EARLY THEORIES ABOUT THE COMPONENTS of personality structure he proposed that the "ego" was not present at birth. Rather he thought it was an acquired derivative of the "collision" between Id energy and Society. The term "Id" designated raw unorganized energy produced by metabolism. Society was understood to exert a restraining and molding effect on the emerging energy, so the Ego was a residue of learned stimulus and response, born of the conflict between Id and Society.

Other theoreticians, including Freud's daughter, Anna, brought to psychoanalysis an expanded ego-psychology which insisted that the ego was an original structure, not merely acquired. The names of Hartmann, Kris, and Lowenstein are associated with that later psychoanalytic school which spoke of "an autonomous conflict-free sphere of the ego." Autonomous (inherent) functions of the Ego include perception, sensation, experiential learning, and object-relating outreach.

The cellular model takes for granted the real presence of the Ego at birth. And in that model maturation of the Person is essentially maturation of the Ego. The Ego is not only the teachable student in the Person; it is also the Explorer and the Experimenter, autonomously reaching out into the environment with curiosity and with zest for relationship. The timetable for the unfolding maturation of the Ego is established by the nuclear Self, whereas the education of the Ego depends on its actual experience with the Environment.

The Ego is the organ of exchange with the Environment. Just as the cellular limiting membrane "knows" what is nutritious and what is toxic for the cell, so the Ego recognizes what is healthy and what is unhealthy for its person. Among the crucial sentinel agents safeguarding the Person's health and growth is the human immune system. In health immunity functions in a simple binary fashion, distinguishing among environmental objects "Friend" or "Foe" and alien or congenial. The apertures of the cellular membrane and of the Ego open to health and close to unhealth; they also serve to expel toxic intake or toxic wastes. Under adverse environmental conditions, the immune system and the Ego's other defenses can be lulled into inadequate responsiveness (under-reaction) by overload or overpromise, and they can be provoked into excessive responsiveness (over-reaction) by startle or by stimulation which is unpredictable.

In healthy child-rearing, the containing parental environment does not impose that which is alien to the child's Ego. Natural parents mainly nudge and gently restrain to protect the child and to teach consensus values. Parents who trust the child's natural affinity for health will teach self-discipline and self-reliance by patient repetition and regularity, assured that the child's Ego wants to build-in those functions. The child who learns self-discipline can close his Ego against environmental danger and can open it judiciously to emerging narcissistic energy. The developing Ego progressively converts impulsivity into spontaneity.

Whereas the Self is timeless and ageless, the Ego is the repository of continuity-in-time and of experiential memory.

When a person, especially a young one, suffers injury or threat or loss, the Self-part experiences the emotional response as "forever." It is the Ego which reminds the Self and the Person of remedial options and of recovery. Those reminders, along with the sense of containment, supply Self-soothing for the traumatized person. If on the other hand the Ego is ill-developed or weakened by stress, unable to provide sufficient soothing and reassurance, then the injured person will respond with panic or sustained anxiety.

Development of the self-soothing function, which is a prerequisite for continued maturation, illustrates the crucial influence of healthy parenting on the child's Ego. A self-soothing Ego emerges only as a child experiences from the parental environment consistent truthful assessment of danger or injury and accurate prediction of recovery. The child's Ego does not learn to soothe if the parental environment regularly exaggerates or minimizes the extent of injury or illness. The natural parent who holds and comforts and reassures the injured child understands intuitively that this occasion is an opportunity for the child to build-in self-soothing capacity. A self-absorbed parent is more likely to experience the child's injury as an inconvenience or as an occasion for blame, at best "something to be gotten over with." Inadequate self-soothing capacity renders the developing person susceptible to the use of addictive substances (food, sweets, alcohol, drugs) or addictive behaviors (sexual promiscuity, money-making, money-spending, gambling, speeding).

Recall that the containing boundary of the cell is called the limiting membrane; its counterpart in the Person is the Ego. The human ego throughout life exerts a limiting function. In health, the Ego limits the quantity and quality of commodities and energies entering the cell. As well it limits the amount of energy expended from the Self into the Environment. The healthy Ego can say "No!"

The Ego not only contains and protects and defends; it also learns and refines and expands. The Self can choose and the Ego can execute a tremendous number of activities, ranging in skill from competence to virtuosity. Language acquisition, fine motor control, model-making, muscle-building, music-making, rhythmical movement, artistic creation, aesthetic pleasure, athletic and acrobatic feats, varieties of play, and routinized work are just a few possibilities. For fulfillment one's Ego needs disinterested assistance and training from the parental environment and inspiration from one's Self.

As the organ of exchange the Ego is also the organ of adaptation. The capacity to adapt to an almost infinite number of environmental conditions and requirements both enriches and endangers the human animal. The person must have its basic dependency needs (food, shelter, and recognition) met regularly in order to survive. In order to obtain those needs the adapting Ego negotiates and compromises with less-than-ideal environmental providers. From such environments the individual's Ego learns how much abuse, toxicity, falsehood, and inattention it is *able* to accept in order to have basic needs met. And the person learns how much unhealth the Self is willing to accept. Unfortunately in the Ego's experience of adaptation, that which is tolerable comes to be that which is expectable. It is this very capacity to adapt and survive in unhealthy environments that allows the child to collude in creating a False Self system.

Chapter 8

Notes On The Environment

FOR ANY SINGLE HUMAN ANIMAL, THE ENVIRONMENT IS EVERY thing else, near and far, in the universe. It includes other people, the artifacts and manufacts of civilization, and all of nature. Nature includes all flora and fauna, the solid and watery earth itself, the atmosphere, and such dynamic phenomena as climate, weather, earthquakes, and meteor showers.

If Freud's early idea about the Ego's origin was incorrect, his understanding of the vast influence of the Environment on that Ego was not overdrawn. The molding of the Ego by the Environment is not absolute but the effect is enormous and highly predictable. Human beings raised in rural rhythms and in close kinship to nature have different perspectives and even different personalities from their city-dwelling kin. However far-removed from the native habitat, the human animal will probably always respond more healthfully to the honking of migratory geese than to the honking of impatient taxi drivers.

Winston Churchill is included in the roll of those who testify to the power of the environment. During the early years of World War II the British House of Commons was destroyed by German bombing. There was protracted debate as to whether the rebuilt structure should be a replica of the old or a new more spacious and modern building. In his persuasive concluding speech on behalf of replication, Churchill declared, "We shape our buildings, and afterwards they shape us." The same could be said about societies and families.

In elementary biology the student learns about the effects of the liquid environment on suspended cells. Whenever the concentration of ions, say of sodium or chloride, is different within the cell from that concentration in the outside liquid, there is an electrochemical movement to equilibrate the inside and outside. (Nature abhors imbalance as well as vacuum). That equilibration is achieved by movement of ions and water through the openings in the semi-permeable membrane of the cell's container. A more concentrated (hypertonic) environmental liquid will "draw" water from within the cell and "send" ions into it; the reverse of those movements applies for a less concentrated (hypotonic) environment, with liquid moving into the cell. If balance cannot be achieved in the first instance the cell will shrink; if it cannot occur in the second case the cell will explode.

Interaction between the cell and the liquid environment is paralleled for the individual person in respect to different types of environment. The human's environment can be said to be "hypertonic" (excessive) or "hypotonic" (deficient) in respect to activity, energy, noise, light, attention, expectation, and so on. In general human animals exposed to environments which are "too much" shrink into apathy, demoralization, and withdrawal. And those exposed to deficient environments tend toward restlessness, desperation, and violent engagement. These truisms apply to the prevailing environment in which the individual lives. The generalizations do not hold within the closer family environment where so many other variables determine a child's inclination toward apathy or violence.

While nature and the general society exert substantial

influence on the development of the particular child's Ego, those factors pale in comparison to the molding power within the family-of-origin. Specific restrictions, taboos, preferences, and emphases are established by the family's system of rewards and punishments. Not only are there common instructions which apply to all the children but also specific rôles are assigned to individual children. Typical rôles are Peacemaker, Agitator, Warrior, Problem-Child, Scapegoat, Standard-bearer, Healer, Helper, or Savior. Ethics, morals, and values are adopted by the developing Ego mainly in response to modeling by parents and other significant adults. Particular interests in literature, music, cooking, athletics, or crafts are also frequently sparked by models.

Amongst the many species, the human animal has a singularly lengthy maturational period, from birth to age fourteen or thereabouts. The basic characteristics of the Ego are established during that time of concurrent progressive growth and extended exposure to the "home" environment. In a very real sense the individual's Ego is a replica of the parentified environment. The child will become, in great measure, what the child is exposed to. And modeling behavior is vastly more influential than advice, instruction, warnings, promises, or other verbal transmissions.

To repeat an earlier association, the healthy parental container conveys healthy influence to the child's Ego by modeling reliability, regularity, patient repetition (practice), initiative, and truthfulness. Those factors converge and meet in the quality of discipline. A disciplined parental container teaches self-discipline to the child's Ego. Self-discipline is the prerequisite for transforming impulsivity into spontaneity. Impulsivity is an eruption of energy through a weak or weakened Ego. Spontaneity is the consummation of awareness.

And sensory awareness can flourish only under the watchfulness of a flexible and sturdy Ego, an Ego friendly both to the Self and to the environment.

If the Ego's characteristics are imparted during the maturational phase they are certainly not permanently cemented. Throughout life the Ego will continue to progressively resemble any prevailing environment to which it has prolonged exposure. In early life an unhealthy parental container imparts an unhealthy Ego; a healthy container co-creates a healthy Ego for the child. Regardless of the quality of a child's early start in life, it is always true that a healthy organism cannot remain healthy in an unhealthy environment. Either one must re-structure that environment or leave it if one is to maintain health. Restructuring of an unsatisfactory environment means reducing toxic content (smog, acid rain, discounts, passivity, or abuse) or imparting missing needs (balanced dietary, companionship, sunlight, affection, and intellectual or sensory stimulation).

No single environmental commodity is more crucial to the developing child's Ego than that of *emotion* (or affect). A child's early interpersonal environment has an emotional tone (excitable, calm, flat), an emotional flavor (sad, happy, fearful, angry), and emotional "rules." By "rules" I mean the modeling of emotional expression, especially by the parents or surrogates. The sum of those modeling expressions are implicitly taught as "the way to feel." Under stress some adults mainly express fear; others anger, others sadness. Some grow quiet, some get noisy. In some families angry expression is not allowed; in others it is both modeled and encouraged. Sadness or fear might be outlawed, but then only driven underground. Guilt-induction and shame-infliction are the two common control programs in families and sub-cultures; they leave powerful residues.

Part of the emotional education of the young Ego is interactional. Emotional interaction is observed and experienced. The child observes, for instance that when father expresses anger toward mother, she gets sad. And the child experiences fear in himself when either parent or any adult expresses anger toward him. Thus there develop paired emotions: anger with fear, anger with sadness, fear with shame, happiness with fear, happiness with guilt, and so on. These paired responses are established as reflex expectations in the developing Ego and they will be projected into later relationships if unexamined. One of the exciting and enlivening discoveries for a person in psychotherapy is couched in the exclamation, "Gosh! I never knew you could have a different feeling about that!"

Shame is such a powerfully influential emotion that it needs special commentary. Unlike guilt which issues from that "outermost superego layer" of the Ego, shame strikes the very center of the Person, the Self. Recall that I proposed earlier that the Self has no need from the environment except reflection. But the need for reflection is a crucial one for the Person. Reflection establishes *image*. If I am shamed by "them" or ashamed of myself, my self-esteem plummets. So shaming and teasing are especially injurious transactions, withering self-esteem and spawning impotent rage, a seed-bed for revenge. The gravity of shaming is minimized by the common protest, "You hurt my feelings." But there is actually no such thing as "hurt feelings." It is the Self/Soul/Spirit which is hurt by shaming. The wounded Soul does accurately report the "feeling of hurt" however.

The shaming person might say "I am so ashamed of you" or "You should be ashamed" (adding guilt to shame). But the commonest vehicle of shame is the use of categorical labels:

"You are a bad person"; "You are lazy/rotten/liar/sneak/ superficial, etc."

To some extent the hurtful effects of unhealthy emotional modeling and teaching are reduced in extended families or sub-cultures where a particular style, such as shaming or expressing anger loudly, is done in common. Emotional hurts are less damaging to the Self if they can be taken less personally because "everybody is doing it." That truism accounts for the observation that children raised in "shame cultures" do not automatically reflect the stigmata of personally absorbed shame.

Finally a particular developmental phase is seen as a critical environmental shaper of emotional life and of Ego maturity. The term "rapprochement" is used by the developmental theorists to indicate the toddler phase and its opportunity for social relatedness. The French word rapprochement means "the state or establishment of cordial relationships," according to Webster. That is an optimistic hope for a developmental phase so fraught with injurious possibilities. Whatever quality characterizes that phase for the child largely determines lifelong styles and qualities of separation and attachment.

The toddler, or "floor baby," has grown sufficiently to leave the nest of hands-on containment, the orbit of the "lap baby." She literally moves away from the mothering person or persons to explore the world. She crawls and toddles toward shiny or strangely-textured objects, satisfying the Ego's outreaching curiosity by handling and mouthing everything in sight. Early in the phase her forays are short-lived. She is rather quickly filled with stimulation and then needs close containment again. She calls to "mother" visually or verbally or moves back to home-base on her own. The mothering person may or may not be ready for the child's return; as well, she may or may not have been ready for her departure. The attitude of the mothering person about the toddler's comings and goings imparts to the young Ego lifelong expectations and styles in the crucial matters of separation and attachment. The child who toddles away from an anxiously clinging mother-person has her curiosity and zest blunted by concern for the adult's welfare. On the other hand if the caregiver mainly wants to be rid of responsibility for the child, then the toddler's development is impeded by concern for her own welfare and survival.

Ideally the mothering person would be the biological mother and she would be regularly at home with the toddler. The mother would understand the enormous impact of the rapprochement phase and she would plan to make the most of the opportunity, essentially devoting that year to the child. She would maintain a disinterested delight in the toddler's rich adventures and she would submit to the child's unpredictable initiative in leaving and returning. She would "go on about" her other business when the toddler moved from her presence. She would delight in the child but continue to entertain herself. And, of crucial importance, she would not depend on the child for her primary interpersonal support. Such an ideal is not likely to be met, but any approximations in principle prepares the child to live well domestically and vocationally.

Regardless of the quality and outcome of the rapprochement phase, the legacy of the recipient Ego is either anxiety and distance or confidence and intimacy. The developmentalists have proposed the idea that two "mothers" are incorporated in the Ego's experience: one, the close-up "object-mother," and the other the non-visible "environmental mother." According to that notion, each of us carries in our consciousness an expectation of how he/she/they will feel about me when I am present and while I'm away. Will I be "out of sight, out of mind?" Or will my spouse/child/friend/colleague keep me comfortably in mind in my absence and welcome my return? If I cannot separate with confidence that the mothering-other (spouse/colleague/friend) will maintain the home or work environment, then I will attach too tightly. And if my returns are met with criticism or expressions of neediness then I will find ways to extend the separation un-naturally. Can I expect the environmental-other to take good care of himself/herself during my absence or will I worry about that other's welfare and check-in frequently, in my head or by telephone? The variables and the vicissitudes of the rapprochement phase are indeed determinative.

And the influence and shaping effects of the Environment continue throughout one's life as a major determinant of the quality of that life.

Chapter 9

Two False Self Systems: Tom's And Sandra's

THE STORIES OF TOM AND SANDRA ILLUSTRATE THE COMMON origin of all False Self Systems. But the two particular stories represent quite different wrinkles on the common pattern.

The False Self System is not entirely false and certainly not entirely unhealthy. The establishment of the false system is inevitable for socialized individuals and collectives. The system develops as a compromise between conflicting self-willed parties of unequal power (e.g. infant and parent, individual and society, terrorist and target victims, male and female, employer and employee, etc.)

The central falsehood and common origin of the False Self System lie in the substitution of an outside Self as the unnatural director of the individual's personhood. That outside-Self is the self-interested narcissistic sector of a parent, or surrogate, or larger parental structure.

The child is willing and able to collude in the surrender-and-takeover only because he gets benefits and rewards which do meet some of his basic needs, albeit only partially. In order to safeguard their basic dependency relationships most children have to "swallow" a lot that is not good (healthy) for them, and they have to do without a lot which they need and deserve.

Unfortunately the adaptable Ego can adapt to a minimally healthy dietary and it can swallow things lock, stock, and barrel in the service of survival. During the prolonged period of dependent maturation, the adapting child progressively loses its powers of discrimination. So by the time he reaches biological maturity in late teenage, the person no longer distinguishes clearly between his will and the incorporated-other's will, between his own thoughts and the incorporated "voices" of the outside directors, or between his dreams for himself and the swallowed assignments of others.

Tom's False Self System was based on compliance and the suppression of anger. In contrast Sandra's system was based on defiance and it was characterized by fixed and acutely erupting anger. Compliance and defiance are both reactions to another's initiative and they are the twin behaviors of the False Self System. Tom and Sandra were wounded early and frequently by parental containers which were impositional more than empathic and neglectful more than attuned. These woundings occurred in two families-of-origin who were "mainly good" people. They were also "good-hyphen-evil people, the most hurtful of all."

I have borrowed the language of Tom's dream to emphasize the "mixed-bag" nature of the False Self System. The configurations in that dream are also remarkably apt illustrations of the false system. The small glass house containing the "good" people can be understood either as a True Self-directed individual in a False Self society or as Tom's (the individual's) True Self being pressured by an oppressively overwhelming (Super) Ego.

Now I'll extract Tom's term "evil" and translate the concepts of evil, sin, and bad in the language of my cellular model. Here I am pointing to nothing less that the central problem of the human personality.

Tom and Sandra and I were all reared under varying degrees of influence by the Judeo-Christian mind-sets. Terms like evil and sin were at least as palpable as the concepts of gravity and thermodynamics. On a given day they were also equally irrelevant to one's private concerns. And even though all of us raised under the Biblical pillar and cloud had to worry sometimes about whether we were "good boys" or "good girls," I am presently grateful for the introduction of the categories of good and evil. I believe that if we do not ponder and wrestle with the basic reality of everyman's and everywoman's destructiveness then we are left only to address symptoms.

The symptoms of unhealth for the human animal, for the False Self System, range from teasing to terrorizing, from procrastination to betrayal, from snide sarcasm to suicide, from self-righteousness to rape, from insensitivity to larceny, and on and on and on.

The disease of human destructiveness from which the symptoms arise can be described in the vocabulary of the cellular model. Within the individual and within Society symptoms of unhealth and signs of injury occur when there is an imbalance between Self-interest and Ego-interest. When one person invests excessive (unbalanced) energy in a private agenda, he will inevitably injure the people in his Ego-object-relating environment by "using" them or neglecting them. On the other side if a person invests excessive energy in "serving" others, neglecting his healthy self-interest, he will become depressed and eventually embittered.

Tom's parents provided essentially healthy containment for their young sons. They were able to do that because they too had inherited and maintained healthy containment by the concentric encirclements of extended family, numerous friendships, and a larger local society which was industrious, relatively classless, and homogenous in values.

Sarah, Tom's mother, provided as well the germs of False Self Systems for the sons. Her personhood was unbalanced with excessive energy in her caregiving Ego, to the neglect of her own Self-expression. With unplanned inevitability she sought self-fulfillment vicariously in the accomplishments, achievements, and status of her three men. And Sarah's surrender to the initiative of her men is the distaff companion of her moral domination which forced some surrender by the men. That oscillating sequence of domination and submission is characteristic of life in the False Self System, both for the individual and for the sub-group. Sarah also contributed to the fabric of Tom's false system by fabrication of his worth. Sometimes she elevated him to grandiose stature as her "wonderful little man" ("I couldn't get along without you.") and sometimes she relegated him to second-class status or eliminated him completely with her silence.

His father supported Tom as advocate, encourager, and unconditional approver but he exploited their friendship. From a too-early age Tom was his father's domestic confidante, receiving complaints about Sarah that Father should have directed to her. And within the assumed bounds of "affectionate" teasing John, Sr. labeled Tom as clumsy and bumbling.

Tom's own collusive contributions to this False Self System included a repertoire of self-discounting clowning behaviors, blame detection, sly slander, odious comparison, and a self-effacing self-righteousness. With numerous available models he became a manipulative master of the cycle of guilt, confession, and restoration.

Unlike Tom, who was reared in a homogeneous majority culture, Sandra was distinctly in the minority as black, part Indian, and female. Rather than having the comfort and safety of a friendly holding container, Sandra was required by early circumstance to develop hypervigilance and suspicious mistrust of an alien majority. Sandra's Ego, regardless of the quality of her family life, was shaped substantially by the structural disharmony between her blackness and the surrounding whiteness of the dominant culture. Sandra was a typical victim of racism, which is one of the major symptoms of the larger Societal False Self System. Another such symptom is poverty. All the gulfs and barriers of race and class involve an imbalance in alleged personal worth, in influence, and in power. Individuals and sub-groups who are oppressed by the dominant culture react by compliance ("Yes, sir"), or by passive-aggressive behavior ("Maybe"), or by defiance ("No!"). Sandra defied and attacked the false systems in her environment and in her family. She also complied with the educational system and she passive-aggressively acted out her sexual revenge.

Sandra's parents adapted to an oppressive society in which they were implicitly viewed as racially inferior. They preached "Christian forgiveness of white people" and therein established grounds for moral superiority. That internal adjustment to external subjugation is characteristic of society's victims. It can be a springboard for True Self recovery in realistic spirituality, or it can extend the False Self System in prideful self-righteousness and plans for revenge. In Sandra's story we see that initially she "recovered" through False Self extension ("beating them at their own game"), but that later in psychotherapy she was able to make a True Self recovery.

The lines of development of the False Self system begin to emerge. Unbalanced environments produce unbalanced families who raise unbalanced children. The basic imbalance in all those sectors is an unhealthy disproportion between Ego-energy and Self-energy.

Characteristics of False Self Systems are: reactivity, passivity, passive-aggressiveness, winning-and-losing, domination and submission, scorekeeping, odious comparison, indirectness, ulterior motive, manipulation, scheming, revenge, violence, destructiveness towards oneself and others, mood disorders, magical thinking, discounts, exaggerations, and denial. The interlocking relationship between these "building-blocks" of the False Self System will be examined in a later section.

The familiar and ubiquitous operation of the False Self System is illustrated by a brief moment in the story of Sandra's therapy. Recall that early in the group Sandra and Millie had paired affectionately. Then, when Sandra suddenly turned on judgmental Millie, the group acted as if that had not happened. Denial is the typical first-order response of the Ego surprised or shocked in a social context. The collusion of silence was broken several sessions later (long after Sandra's intimate disclosures) only by my confrontive inquiries. Denials and collusive silences are hallmarks of "dysfunctional families" and of "co-dependent relationships," two sub-sets of False Self Systems.

Chapter 10

GENERAL SYSTEMS THEORY AND LIFE-COURSE MODELS

(A) *General Systems*

THERE IS A FIELD OF SCIENTIFIC PHILOSOPHY KNOWN AS General Systems Theory, associated primarily with the name of Ludwig von Bertalanffy.[5] The general systems encompassed by the theory include all levels, from atomic particles through galaxies. Some systems are *closed*, like atoms and crystals and machines; and some are *open*, like viruses and cells and families. The laws governing closed systems are quite different from those which apply to open systems.

A brief introduction to systems theory is important because of its relevance to the operations of the False Self System (which is closed) and the True Self System (which is open).

In a very real sense the False Self System can be understood as a counter-natural imposing of closed system laws onto open living systems or vice versa. Consider those effects as applied to human individuals, families, and societies!

A closed system is well-illustrated by the operation of a heating utility which involves a furnace and a thermostat. If you want the ambient temperature to be 68°, the thermostat signals (sends information to) the furnace which ignites and emits heat until the set temperature is reached at the thermostat. Thereupon the thermostat "tells" the furnace to turn off. This familiar operation highlights the characteristics and the language of closed systems. In all such systems there is a "set point." The system cannot operate with approximations; the set-point must be "just right" or "Perfect." (Closed systems operate by information exchange which is called "feedback." When the set-point has been met the system is said to be in "homeostasis.")

The entire universe is made up of only three forms of "substance": energy, matter (or material), and information. Closed systems are closed to the introduction of anything new in the way of matter or energy; they receive and exchange information only. Open living systems are open to information, matter, and energy. Indeed the intake and output of all three "substances" is necessary for the life and development and growth of living systems (e.g. a flea, a flower, an elephant, a society, a child).

For machines and other closed systems, repair, maintenance, and replacement of worn parts must come from outside the system. In contrast open systems are self-repairing (healing) and self-rejuvenating. They replace their worn parts (e.g. spent cells) from *inside*, while exchanging basic commodities with the environment. Whereas living systems move toward fulfillment (blossoming of a flower, maturation of a person), closed systems move toward "entropy" (wearing out and breaking-down, while performing in exactly the same way all the time).

The primary values for closed systems are *efficient function* and *maximum yield.* Closed systems require control, uniformity, exactness, predictability, and repetition of fixed operations. They are mechanistic, digital, sequential, and linear. Closed system operations are appropriate to building a house, launching a rocket, and establishing law and order. There are indispensable closed system operations within all open systems (e.g. increased heart rate in low-oxygen environments, production of botanical anti-freeze in cold weather blossoms, course-corrections for migratory birds, and "control" of the flow of hormones by the pituitary gland). Closed systems however cannot tolerate open systems. The introduction of matter or energy causes malfunction in a closed system.

Open system values are primarily *growth* and *fulfillment.* Open systems are vitalistic rather than mechanistic. Their components are individually unique and they operate within a workable range called a "steady state," rather than hewing to a set-point. The vocabulary of open systems is itself rejuvenating: the characteristic operations are trial-and-error, experiment, false start, overshoot, steady-state balance, and equifinality (which means, "There are lots of different ways to get from here to there").

Obviously there are far-reaching implications in general systems theory for the projects of child-rearing, gardening, education, community-building, and psychotherapy.

Children are wounded and False Self Systems are spawned when the natural laws of natural systems are ignored or violated. Parents who trust the native wisdom of the child's Self will allow for trial-and-error, false start, and overshoot. They will also encourage experimentation and they will support equifinality. But they will also be faithful to the closed system requirements of regularity, repetition, and discipline. As indicated earlier, open-system spontaneity can arise only from within the structure of closed self-discipline.

There is a natural order in life which is expressed in rhythm and harmony and balance. The universe is the ultimate Open System, containing both open system and closed system operations, each appropriate to its purpose. Parallel to the healthy balance between Self-energy and Ego-energy is the balance between open and closed systems. Free-will allows the human animal to ignore and violate the laws of nature. Open systems can be stunted by closed system imposition (e.g. perfectionism, control, and force-fitting). Healthily appropriate closed systems can be disrupted by the introduction of open system commodities (e.g. excitement, prejudice, disappointment, intuition, spontaneity, or the assertion of uniqueness).

Dismantling one's own False Self System and rebuilding the True Self System are the goals of psychotherapy and the prerequisites for human fulfillment. Individuals in the False Self System open and close according to external instructions. The recovered True Self System opens and closes on instructions from the interior Self after appraisal of the external environment has been made by the Ego.

In the False Self System, individual human animals become irritable, angry, impatient and frustrated after exceeding their limits in closed system operations (e.g. repetitive work on the assembly line, "controlling" misbehavior, or imposing education on the resistant). They then impulsively explode and "throw a monkey-wrench into the machinery" or "gum up the works." On the other hand if the individual fails to guard his boundaries and indulges in pseudo-open permissiveness, letting others exceed his limits, he will again explode in violent expression.

When the True Self is restored as the legitimate "ruler," the person restores balance and rhythm and harmony. She respects boundaries and sovereignty, her own and others'. She does not stay too long at the machine, and she does not flinch from prolonged interpersonal responsiveness.

(B) *Life Course Models*

While the primary containing adults are rearing their children as best they can or as minimally as they must, they are also constantly teaching the child particular perspectives on life and society. Simultaneously the dominant culture and the local sub-group culture are indoctrinating with their perspectives, which may or may not be like those of the child's family.

These concentric perspectives obviously condition the child to certain attitudes and expectations. It makes a substantial difference in the child's life if he is taught, "Life is a beautiful gift," rather than "Life is a vale of tears — burden — trial — unfair — dangerous, etc."

The imprinting messages about "How life is" are transmitted mainly by the parents' behaviors and emotional responses. They are also conveyed verbally by pronouncements, sayings, proverbs, and directives. Common messages include:

"Take care of number one!"
"It's dog-eat-dog out there."
"All politicians are corrupt."
"If you want it done right, do it yourself."
"Do unto others as you would have them do unto you."
"You will get your reward in heaven."
"You can be anything you want to be."
"Success is mainly a matter of luck."
"Just have faith."
"Don't trust a stranger."
"Birds of a feather flock together."
"Human nature doesn't change."
"You can't legislate morality."
"Might makes right."

"A soft answer turneth away wrath."

"Extra sweat makes extra money."

"Idleness is the devil's workshop."

"The rich get richer and the poor get poorer."

"Just be happy."

"Suffering builds character."

"Don't play until all your work is finished."

"Eat, drink, and be merry, for tomorrow we may die."

"People stay the way they're born; you can't change."

"All things are possible to those who love the Lord."

"Most poor people are just lazy bums."

"Blessed are those who are persecuted for righteousness'
      sake."

"You've made your bed, now lie in it."

"Everyone will let you down sooner or later."

"You can find something good in everybody."

Many children were told, "Sticks and stones can break your
bones, but words can never hurt you." That falsehood is
illuminated by the litany above, with its combination of
discounts, grandiosities, limitations, half-truths, prejudices, and,
contradictions.

There are three unhealthy models of "How life is"
commonly held up to children by the dominant society. They
are all closed-system models. I call them The Progress Model,
The Puritan Model and The Heroic Model.

Fig. 5 The Progress Model

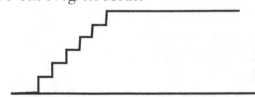

This model is frequently presented as a staircase with an accompanying timetable of "normal" development or advance. "By age six months the child should be doing. . . ." "By age thirty you should be . . .", etc., etc. As with all closed-system models, both the picture and the timetable are imposed from the outside.

Implied in the staircase progress model is the expectation that one should reach a certain step at a predetermined (set-point) time. Also implicit is the promise that one will someday reach a landing at the top, a point of "arrival."

If one's movement is delayed or interrupted he is frequently urged to hurry and catch up. Catching up refers to some arbitrary "Table of Normal Development" or to the faster pace of a peer climber or both.

Progress is a hazardous term when applied to human animals and other living systems. Progress is measurable movement toward a discrete goal or end-point. As such it is the appropriate concept in projects such as weight loss or gain, increasing aerobic capacity, or physical rehabilitation. But the person, like the universe, is basically on open system which contains some closed system operations. Self-measurement promotes self-consciousness, which reduces spontaneity and enrichment. Like flowers, persons blossom and grow and become who they uniquely are.

Fig. 6 The Puritan Model

The Puritan Model is represented by a straight line connecting two set-points, the starting-point (birth) and the end-point (death).

In this model the child is set on "the right track" in earliest life and the learned goal is to stay "on course." The puritan's characteristics are consistency, predictability, regularity, strong will-power , and resistance to temptation. The puritan monitors and corrects all deviations, his own and those of others. Validation of one's worth is tentative and probationary and is measured primarily in the avoidance of error.

Fig. 7 The-Heroic Model

The Heroic Model is well represented by Sisyphus in Greek mythology. Sisyphus was sentenced by the gods to perpetually push a boulder up a hill and then at the point of inertia to lower it again. As with the staircase model there is the illusion that there's a flat resting place just a bit farther up the hill. "Try a little harder, Sisyphus!"

The weight of the boulder and the incline of the hill are such that it is impossible for one person to push it higher. The illusory hope of pushing the boulder of one's problems to the plateau eventually fades, and the hero refuses to ask another person for help. So the heroic struggle gives way to heroic resignation, with the later compensation of a triumphant funeral and perhaps an afterlife of posthumous admiration.

Eventually most people come to recognize that these closed-system models are false. It is that recognition more that any hormonal or aging factor that accounts for "mid-life crisis."

A person disenchanted with society's imposed models will frequently adopt one of three subjective models based on his experience. Those models-by-default are named Roller-Coaster, Cynical, and Discontinuous; as a group they are called "secondary models."

The *Roller Coaster Model* of "How life is" results from the lingering effort to please and to still conform to a habituated model that no longer has credibility. The subjective alternation between conformity and non-conformity translates into alternating perceptions of success or failure, optimism or pessimism, and elation or depression.

The *Circular Model* is the conclusion of cynicism. The life course is perceived as round-and-round, superficial, flat, and repetitively going "nowhere."

The *Discontinuous Model* is one which renounces all goals, meanings, continuity, and structure. Life is simply moment-to-moment experience. Dependency is denied and the prevailing attitude toward the environment is indifference. The life-style in that model is impoverished and ill-nourished; it invites the use of alcohol and drugs.

These "secondary" models are fall-back positions for persons who earlier had "bought" society's closed-system models. For poor people, oppressed minorities, and anti-social families the secondary models are the only ones available from earliest life.

The *Healthy Model* is a template from one's True Self and from the natural world. It is represented pictorially by the configuration of a helix, a structure which is continuous but open-ended, three-dimensional, and expansively growthful. It is an open system. (A detailed description of the Helical Model will be given in the last chapter.)

If a parent or teacher or psychotherapist conceptualizes "life" in the pattern of one or more of the closed-system models his response to the developing or wounded animal will be activistic, impositional, interventional, and corrective.

On the other hand if the containing person understands "life" as grounded in the self-regulating, self-repairing, open-systemness of the human animal, the response will be attendant, attuned, consultative, patient, and trustful of the other's native health.

Chapter 11

AL'S BURDEN: THE MISSING LINC

WHEN HE CALLED FOR AN APPOINTMENT HE SAID HIS NAME was Al Burbank. His long-time individual therapist had suggested that it might be useful for him to join one of my therapy groups. With a thin laugh he added, "I have a social phobia and it has recently come back in spades."

Al arrived early for that first appointment. Marianne, my office manager, asked him to fill out the standard information sheet in the waiting room. Ordinarily I pick up that sheet from her desk when I go out to meet the new person. But on this occasion she brought it to my office and handed it to me, smiling with something close to delight. Marianne's love of the human animal and her appreciation of the unusual are important healing elements in the therapeutic container which is my workplace. Just the day before Marianne and I had been talking together about the variable fate which hangs on a given name. Her ethnic names are regularly mispronounced so she is sympathetic as well as interested in the vicissitudes of name-choosing. She said simply, "Look at this."

In the limited space following the line-item, "Name," Al had written almost a paragraph over and around his formal ABRAHAM LINCOLN BURBANK, in bold block letters. Scribbled around that pronouncement like graffiti were an assortment of options: Abe, Ab, A. L., Linc, Mr. Lincoln, Ford's, Burp and Al, with comments about their origins.

When Al came into my office I noticed that this tall gangly man had a certain gracefulness about him, a giraffe-like combination of awkwardness and coordination. Also that behind his anxious furtive hunted-animal look was a centered strength and serenity.

Al launched immediately if haltingly into his "presenting complaint." About a month ago he had attended his twentieth high school reunion, mainly at the urging of his wife who went with him. He had had a "terrible" time there, he said. "It brought back so much of the pain of my childhood. I was humiliated all over again. Then I felt angry at Ann for pushing me to go and angry at myself for not knowing better."

Looking directly at me for the first time, Al smiled slightly and pointed to the information sheet on the small table by my chair. "I guess you saw all that stuff I wrote about my names."

"I was sorta surprised that all of that came pouring out, but I wasn't surprised either. Most of the people at the reunion remembered me as "Linc." A couple of them even made the predictable bad joke about the 'missing Linc' being found. None of those people seemed malicious. They laughed and I laughed with them, just the way I used to, and I hated myself for that."

After returning home from the reunion, Al was anxious and depressed. He felt panicky in public places which had previously been comfortable for him. He resumed old patterns of avoidance and excuse-making. "I'm really discouraged. I'm almost forty and I thought I was over all that stuff."

"Ann got really upset too," he continued. "She must've been embarrassed about me and for me. She knew I was angry with her. She felt guilty, and then mad at me for being mad at her. Anyway she has gone back to see her therapist. He prescribed some tranquilizers for Ann. She told me with what I took to be straight humor that he had also asked if Dr. Salmon had prescribed anything for my phobia. And I know he knows that Salmon doesn't believe in medication. I thought that was a cheap shot."

Al paused and was quiet. He looked up, more brightly. "That's funny, I mean odd-funny. Just then when I said that Dr. Rhaeder had taken a cheap shot, I suddenly felt a lot better. Hmm. Wonder why?"

I had noticed that although Al had been talking to me very steadily that he had made no effort to enlist me. The allotted time for the session was almost over when he made that observation. "I'm sorry. I have forgotten your name. I do tend to space out when I talk about myself. Dr. Salmon said you would probably prefer to be called by your first name. Is it Bill or Bob?"

Al was the only child born to a mother and father who divorced when he was six years old. "My parents were both strange people, I now know. When I was growing up I thought they were normal and I was the only strange one."

The father Will Burbank was a musician, a sometime composer and an instructor in cello at the nearby university. He loved Americana. He was a Civil War buff who worshipped Abraham Lincoln. Aaron Copland was his musical idol. Al's recollection is that Copland's music was "always blaring from Dad's study." Will did not show much love however for Lila or for Al. When he spoke at all to his wife or son, he was usually critical.

Lila was recalled as a sweet-faced sad-faced mother who was frail-looking but somehow strong, Al thought. She rarely spoke to Will and she never responded out loud to his criticism. She doted on Al from a distance. Lila's well-bred stoicism had been instilled in the aristocratic poverty of her Mississippi home. Her father was a well-known well-traveled ornithologist who spent all the family money "tracking down strange birds in strange lands." Lila worshipped her departed father, who was generally absent and always absent-minded. Lila loved Al and she loved the South. When Al was in college she told him that she thought his father had insisted on giving him "that terrible name" as a mean joke to spite her.

The divorce was cruel. For months before he left, Will openly dated a married colleague in the music department. They later married and continued living in the university community. Al saw his father rarely after that. The contacts were stiff and perfunctory and Al remembers being relieved when they stopped altogether.

Without ceremony or explanation, Lila moved Al into the master-bedroom to occupy one of the two single beds which had "always been there." She brought the double bed from the guest-room in for herself and re-arranged furniture throughout the house, all within the month after Will's departure. Shortly Lila's widowed sister Sally came to live with them. Al added, "It all happened so quickly that I wondered later if Mother and Aunt Sally had been planning that for a long time."

Al began having nightmares. Several times Lila was awakened by his moans and startles. She moved him into the bed with her without waking him. After several weeks he abandoned his single bed and moved into his mother's bed. Al told me that he was pretty sure of all those details because he was just starting school at that time. He recalled that he got "real spacey" and forgetful. His first-grade teacher recommended to Lila that she get professional help for Al because he would frequently "just fog out" during class.

At the child guidance clinic where Al was seen in once-a-week psychotherapy for about two years, he recalls "they all wanted to know a lot about my sleeping in the same bed with Mother. When I first got into therapy with Dr. Salmon a few years ago, he seemed especially interested in all that stuff too."

"So I've talked to a lot of therapists about it because they kept bringing it up. I've tried to remember all I could. I really don't know what I actually remember, what was told to me later by Mother, and what I maybe made up."

"I'm pretty sure that when Mother first moved me and when it became the regular arrangement, we didn't talk about it. It just happened, and I stayed there until I was twelve or thirteen. It always seemed that Mother stayed way over on her side of the bed. If we bumped into each other during the night, she would always move away. I remember wishing she would snuggle with me, but I never asked and she never did."

Al didn't remember much about his therapy at the child-guidance clinic. He always had "men doctors" there and he liked that; they were kind to him. He told me that he did learn at the clinic that he was an "F. L. K." Two residents were talking one day, unaware that he was sitting in the darkened waiting-room. One of them said, in a not-mean way, "In addition to all his other problems Abe is really an F. L.K. - you know, a funny-looking kid." Al commented to me, "That didn't bother me. I already knew I was funny looking."

"Except for my problems with my names and other people's problems with my spacing out, I had a pretty good childhood," Al concluded. "One of the best things was being free to roam around in the woods by myself. I had an imaginary Indian village out there. The people I put in the village became my friends and I could talk to them as myself or I could become one of them."

"Another good thing for me, I realized, was having Aunt Sally live with us. She was fun and she liked to hug me and hold me in her lap. My mother never did that but it seemed like she liked for Aunt Sally to be close to me. Mother and Aunt Sally told me a lot how much I was like their daddy, Grandpa Poole. It seemed like they enjoyed me being spacey and forgetting things. They would look at each other and say, "Isn't that just like him?""

In the sixth grade, Al began to sign his school papers "Linc Burbank." His teacher asked him in private about his name-change. He told her that he was fed up with trying to make Abe and Ab work and he just decided to be "Linc." He had told his mother and she said it would be all right for him to do that. The teacher suggested that she announce the name-change to the class; Al accepted the offer. The announcement was met with some giggling by the classmates but it stopped when the teacher congratulated Al on his courage. By the next day however the nickname "Missing Linc" was being bandied about and it stuck until Al left for college.

Al was the expert on natural science during his school years. He was fascinated with Africa, with the wildlife, with the tall Watusi warriors, and with the long-distance runners of Kenya. He had no close friends but he was widely respected as a "brain" and as a record-setting cross-country track star. During the seventh grade year he came upon a National Geographic article on "the missing link." He told his mother and Aunt Sally that he hoped his class-mates wouldn't see the article. But resourceful Aunt Sally suggested with a laugh that he write his next term-paper on "the missing link" and "beat them to the draw." Al did that and he got an A+ an the paper. The teasing "died down for a while."

After graduating from high school Al attended Antioch College, on the recommendation of his biology teacher. That wise and sensitive person thought the fragile loner he had befriended would be well-served by a school which emphasized independent study and provided the discipline of work-study programs.

During the summer before leaving home for Antioch, the not-so-fragile loner changed his name from Linc to Al.

Al thrived at his well-chosen college. One of his lab partners was a gently assertive girl named Ann who was also a cross-country runner. Before the winter holidays in the freshman year, she asked Al for a supper date. Al told me that although he had never dated before it was easy being with Ann because she seemed so much like Aunt Sally. Al and Ann both majored in biology and graduated with honors. They married during the summer before Al entered graduate school; he would go on to a distinguished academic career in ornithology.

Al's pattern of academic study, of cross-country running, and of courtship were all low-key and matter-of-fact. His style was a carbon copy of Lila's determined ordinariness.

Having had no sexual experience prior to marriage, Al was "disappointed but not surprised" to find himself impotent. He quietly reassured Ann and entered psychotherapy with a university hospital psychiatrist. During the two years of therapy in which he recovered his natural sexuality, Al also learned about the native goodness of anger. Freer to experience his sexuality and his tabooed emotions, Al became less spacey and forgetful. He grew socially more comfortable, if not convivial. As he had somehow managed a "pretty good childhood," so Al had steadily arranged a "good life" in his early adult years. He had a good-enough marriage and a very gratifying career. Along the way Al's self-depreciating humor of his teen-age years had matured to droll irony. Talking about his career as an ornithologist he told me one day with his hint of a smile, "I think I was mainly attracted to birds because of their peculiar names."

The story of Al is the happy story of all people who do better than the experts would have predicted. I have told this story in selective detail to raise the question and suggest some answers: How did this vulnerable fragile injured child turn out so well?

Lila was not demonstrative in her affection but her love and care were constants. Ill-equipped herself for emotional closeness she was able and willing to support Sally's easy warmth with her son. The two sisters together, held up their idealized father as an available male model for Al. The fact that Lila had experienced a rich and respectful relationship with her father conferred far-reaching benefits. Lila was not undone by the meanness and treachery of her husband, and she did not need for Al to become "her man."

Al was introduced early to the healing containers of Mother Nature and of well-attuned psychotherapy, both maternal forces. Both of those exposures reinforced the matter-of-fact realism modeled by his mother. Almost certainly it was Lila's emotional restraint which protected Al from psychological gender confusion. Al's occupancy of his mother's bed was a matter of practicality and Lila did not dramatize the arrangement. Frequently it is the parent's dramatic anxiety which injures the child more than does a particular behavior.

Here we see well-illustrated the principle of health-in-unhealth. Lila's flatness of expression could have been impoverishing but it was also protective. Lila's endurance was both indomitable and transcendent. That combination safeguarded her and her son against a crippling sense of victimization.

Al did join one of my therapy groups. He terminated with the group's and my endorsement after the relatively short stay of eight months. A veteran of ad hoc psychotherapy, Al used the group experience effectively and his phobic symptoms subsided rather quickly. He discovered, as is usually the case with phobias, that his fear was of his own unexpressed feelings. A new department chairman had recently arrived, bringing plans for radical reorganization along with an irritating personality. He was flippant, sarcastic, and teasing. Not surprisingly his style triggered Al's subterranean anger which he had never allowed toward his father or other male authorities. His early experience with two sturdy women, Lila and Sally, and his work with Dr. Salmon had enabled him to traffic easily in healthy anger with Ann and with peers of both sexes. In the supportive group environment Al was able to confront me on several occasions. Al's acceptance of that challenge and opportunity was pivotal, I believe, in his recovery and further growth.

Chapter 12

THE ARCHITECTURE OF
FALSE SELF SYSTEMS

HUMAN DESTINY IS FULFILLED ONLY IN THE TRUE SELF System. In that system the nuclear Self instructs the person toward self-fulfillment *and* toward empathic caretaking of the interpersonal world and of the natural environment. The twin destinies of the True Self System are balanced and harmonious.

The False Self System is built on a flawed foundation; namely, the substitution of an external director for the natural nuclear self. And although most False Self Systems (individual and collective) use solid construction materials for the superstructure (the person's personality and Ego-equipment), still *every* element of the False Self System is off-center. The system is not plumb, because the foundation is built on the sands of denial and pretense. False Self Systems are by definition unbalanced, excessively self-serving (as with the Dominator) or excessively self-subjugating (as with the Submitter). The Dominator and the Submitter might have equally impressive fittings (intelligence, artistic talent, aesthetic appreciation, "morality," and charm) but they are both off-center. One has only to consider the Mafia, the Ministry, and the Medical profession to recognize that there is sometimes honor among thieves and dishonor among the privileged.

The surrender of initiative which ushers in the individual's False Self is inevitable to some extent for every socialized human animal. The young child's biological dependency and relative vulnerability require submission to the greater strength and experience of the parental environment. Wise parents recognize that necessary compromise and they deliberately help the child to resume initiative as the child matures. However, not many parents are very wise, so most children are manipulated, cajoled, seduced, threatened, bribed, or beaten into a demoralizing submission which leads to passivity.

If unbalanced dependency is the causative agent of the False Self System, then passivity is its chronic infection. Passivity is not defined by inertia of energy, but by the abdication of initiative and responsibility. The varied interpersonal behaviors which qualify as passive include Doing Nothing, Overadapting, Agitating, Paralysis, and Violence.[6] Obviously the observable energy expenditure in those behaviors ranges from minimal to massive, but in common none of them proceeds to a mutually satisfying conclusion. Someone is left dangling—suspended—brooding—second-guessing-obsessing. Passivity is the breeder of "unfinished business."

The interruption and suspension of a natural sequence (feeding, eliminating, mating, playing, problem-solving, negotiating, working, sleeping) by passive disengagement leads to distortions of the body and of body-chemistry as well as to mental confusion and distraction. The long-term effects on the individual's body and physiology will be detailed in a later section.

It all starts early, very early. The seed of the False Self System is planted along with the implantation of the fertilized

egg in the uterine wall. Moreover she who carried the egg and
he who supplied the sperm brought the "unfinished businesses"
of their childhoods to bear upon this conception.

Mother and father have free-will and they are free to wish
upon the fetus:

"I hope he'll be a better baby than Jim was."

"My Dad will be so proud that I'm having a boy."

"This will be the first girl grandchild. She'll be special."

"My God! This is too soon. I wish we'd waited."

"Number Four! Good, I've finally beat my sisters!"

"Dammit! You didn't use your diaphragm. You have to get
    an abortion!"

"Oh, I'm so happy. I hope he grows up to be exactly like
    you, darling."

"I hate to go through this again, but the welfare check is
    growing."

"Thank God! Maybe this will save the marriage."

"We need another girl like a hole in the head."

"That ultra-sound report really depressed me. I don't want
    a boy. I hate men."

"Now I'll have someone to take care of me in my old age."

"I'm going to make sure this child is raised differently from
    the way I was."

"I want to name him Lloyd, and I want him to be just like
    his granddaddy."

"She'll be a pianist."

"I hate that sonofabitch who raped me, but I am determined to raise this baby inside me. It's mine."

"The thought of being a mother terrifies me."

"That guy is headed for the Olympics already!"

"I was hoping for a boy to pass the business on to."

During the nine months, more or less, of gestation the conceptus and fetus is nourished by the maternal circulation which delivers oxygen and foodstuffs. That same circulation also delivers to the developing fetus those endocrine (hormonal) substances which the mother is producing in response to her varying life-circumstances, independent of the pregnancy. Anxiety stimulates particular endocrine response; so does anger; so does depression. The emotional state of the gestational mother, be it episodic or fixed, has a marked effect on the fetal physiology.

If one can account for disposition, personality, energy and character in terms of genetic or biochemical determinism then behavioral responsibility is mitigated. Genetics surely determines eye-color, hair-color, height and some other characteristics, but the individual's personality and character, I contend, are essentially conditioned by one's history. As noted above, that history begins in utero, influenced already by parental expectation, generational family patterns, and maternal physiology.

In most instances the newborn's authority as to its own needs and wants is superceded by parental convenience or by the "how to" of the child-rearing experts. The infant is frequently required to "get on schedule," a schedule established outside the child's rhythmical truthfulness. Regularity and predictability of the child's needs are prized by the caretakers who often mistake a "house-broken" infant for a contented one. The early False Self System is built on such innocent crimes against nature.

In observing parent-infant interaction and in consulting with full-grown former infants, I have devised a fable about the early replacement of the True Self System by the False Self System. It goes like this:

"When the newborn child focuses its eyes for the first time it sees a sign-question stretched across the heavens which reads, 'What do you want?' The child answers with grateful trust, 'Milk, or cuddling, or a change of diapers, or more leg-room for thrashing about. Thank you."

This happy state, life in the Garden, continues for several days, even for several weeks for the fortunate few. But inevitably comes the Fall. One day the blissful child, by now a bit colicky or erratic in sleep pattern awakens, looks skyward and sees another sign, 'What's the matter with you?'"

Met repeatedly with that question, the child soon accepts the presumption of flaw in his own person, independent of the environment. So long as the question goes unchallenged the infant-child-person will devote much of its life-energies to wondering about, worrying about, confessing, explaining, rationalizing, proving otherwise, searching for error, and wilting under the presumption of flaw. In order to forestall the withering unanswerable question, some children become passively inert in order to "not make a mistake." Others elect the opposite course, applying their energies to a perfectionism which is calculated to "cover all the bases."

The process of socialization requires rules which safeguard individual rights and which serve the common good. Those rules are true in the same sense that the rules of gravity and thermodynamics are true; they undergird a True Self System.

Most children have the rules of family and society more imposed upon them than explained to them. And most parents enforce the rules by autocratic force or by pacifying bribe, regularly or occasionally. The child subjected to imposition of rules will respond mainly with compliance or mainly by defiance. As regards surrendering initiative, compliance and defiance are flip-sides of the same coin. Those attitudes and behaviors regarding rules are false; they are building-blocks of the False Self System.

The rules of family and society require individual conformity, but the letter-of-the-law always makes mockery of the spirit-of-the-law. That spirit calls for cooperation, flexibility, and tolerance of individual differences which can be honored even as they are being relinquished to a common goal. Thus a child might be healthfully required to "come to supper" at six o'clock, but he should not be unhealthfully required then to eat if he is not hungry. Insecure parents who do not believe in the health of the human interior (theirs or others') generally resort to CONTROL for the establishment of their law and order. The letter-of-the-law requires unchallenged authority, rigidity, and intolerance of differences.

All parents and all parental structures, to greater or lesser extent, impose Control in the service of functional efficiency. They employ Control in order to teach the child impulse-control and "self-control." Control is a characteristic of closed systems which orient around a "set-point," or the "right way." Control is devoted to the suppression and elimination of deviation, error, or idiosyncrasy. The imposition of Control on living open systems is unhealthy and it is a linch-pin of the False Self System.

The healthy commodity for which Control is an unhealthy replacement is called Power, personal power.

Power is the characteristic of moving energy: of electricity, of flowing river, of wind, of biological impulse. Personal power is channeled through a flexible ego-container which relies on skill rather than control. Personal power is mediated by sensory awareness, delicate touch, fine discrimination, and centered balance. Personal power brings life to the subject and to all those in that person's orbit. Skill is acquired only through a discipline which is regular and repetitive, rather than through control which is regimented and random. Skill can develop only through trial-and-error; control is established by the elimination of error.

Control and perfectionism are False Self behaviors which have been substituted for the power and competence of the original True Self System.

The affective (emotional) life of most children is falsely distorted within the family structure. Children are told not to have feelings they do have ("Don't be angry . . . sad . . . scared . . . jealous, etc.") and to have feelings which are not natural at the moment ("You know you love your brother"; "Be ashamed!", etc.) Similarly, with sensations, there is frequently pressure for uniformity ("You couldn't be cold. The thermostat is at 72°," or "Go ahead and eat some spinach; it tastes good.") Inevitably the child begins to mistrust her natural emotions and sensations or to mistrust the parent, or both. To some extent, large or small, socialization requires self-anesthesia, of simply learning to deny the presence or significance of certain feeling-states. In some families there is a taboo against emotional arousal of any sort

— quiet is good, taciturn is better, stoic is best. In other families serious thoughtfulness is discouraged — inauthentic laughter and forced joviality accompany all verbal exchange. One of those families "makes sense," the other "makes merry," but effectively neither of them "makes contact." Contact is the prerequisite for bilateral enrichment. The False Self System features a full repertoire of contact abortions and deviations which thwart intimacy and growth.

Cognitive (mental, intellectual) functioning is distorted when children are given misinformation, insufficient information, too much information, or false information (lies). Both intellectual life and fantasy life (mental imaging) are corrupted by threat of calamity ("The Judgment Day is coming!") or unrealistic promise ("Some day our ship will come in.")

Mystification discourages curiosity and stunts intellectual development. ("It's simply the will of the Lord"; "Things happen in threes"; "The devil made me do it"; "Well, that's just the way we Libras are"; "You are too young to understand"; "I know it's true because I have a gut feeling about it.")

Magical thinking is normative for small children. In healthy intellectual development it is progressively replaced by scientific cause-and-effect perspectives. The primitive mind exaggerates one's personal influence on the environment, ascribing unrealistic consequence to actions, wishes, or feelings. ("It thundered because I stole a cookie"; "My dog died because I was mad at him"; "If I wish hard enough, I'll get a pony"; "I got polio because I played with myself.") In growthful environments, children are patiently disabused of these false connections, without any ridicule which would discourage the healthy magic of creative fantasy. In controlling environments parents and other authorities induce fearful compliance by reviving and reinforcing the child's magical thinking. ("Your mother left because you're a bad girl"; "If you keep that up, you'll never amount to anything"; "The Jews are being punished because they killed Christ"; "It's bad luck to walk under a ladder.")

Both mystification and magical thinking are extended by the parental practices of mind-reading and motive-reading. ("I know what you're thinking"; "I knew you were going to say that"; "You got sick so you wouldn't have to go to school"; "You don't really love me"; "You enjoy playing pitiful, don't you?") Unfortunately, for confirmation, the mind-readers sometimes guess correctly.

Rationalization is a latter-day derivative of magic and mystification. It provides a spurious explanation, for defensive purposes. Rationalization is encouraged when one is interrogated about motive ("Why did you do that?"). That question is so familiar in family and society that it goes largely unexamined. A closely-related rendition, "Why didn't you think of that earlier?", is but thinly-veiled criticism. For parents, teachers, and spouses there is a pertinent doggerel:

"If you wanta teach someone to lie
All you do is ask them, 'Why?'"

Small children tend to speak plainly and directly. They soon learn that it is safer in society and at home to be less clear, more indirect, and non-committal ("Either one would be all right with me.") Rather than asking for what they want, "polite" children have learned to hint or to signal the other side of a "Yes" or "No" with facial expression and body language. The collusion of indirectness is extended by asking the subtly insulting question "Are you sure?" In response to someone's declarative statement ("I don't want any cake, thank you," or "I believe I'll go to bed"), the other person assumes lack of candor and then asks, "Are you sure?"

All of these ways of speaking and exchanging information in the False Self System take their toll, arousing anger, impatience and, mistrust. Adults frequently complain that in their important relationships at home and work, "We have a communication problem." These people rarely appreciate the magnitude of the "communication problems" taught by families and schools and churches. And, faithful to the teachers of the False Self System, these adult plaintiffs of "communication problems" have falsely located the "problem" within their contemporary relationship, with the chief culprit usually assumed to be the other partner.

Unclear indirect communication serves the False Self System's characteristic ambivalence about separation and attachment. As was the case in unhealthy rapprochement-phase behavior, the parent wants the child to leave and also to stay; the same ambivalence applies to the child whose nuclear Self-director has been co-opted by mistrustful Parents.

It is this ambivalence which underlies the go-stay, push-pull, approach-avoidance, growth-regression awkwardness of the False Self behaviors. If a small child or an adult lover is invited to open-armed contact and then interrupted or turned away, there will be deleterious effects on that person's mind (mental processes), body (musculo-skeletal system), soul (capacities for trust, love, and soothing), and physiology (flow of neuro-endocrine substances and blood chemistry).

When the human animal is reaching out for something wanted or needed in the environment there is an organismic outflow which serves that particular behavior. The muscles and skeletal joints, especially those of the arms, legs, and neck *extend* outward, Simultaneously the tissues are bathed in activating adrenalin-like fluids. Cardiovascular output increases; the pulse rate and blood pressure rise. This reaching-out sequence is called Providing Behavior. The sequence of extension applies to all providing, for oneself or for others.

Once the animal has procured the desired object or commodity from the environment, then a different organismic response is activated to serve intake. The *flexor* muscles, which were neurochemically inhibited during the reaching-out, now become the agents to bring food or information or affection inward for contact and consummation. The posture and neurochemistry of consummation is the opposite of that for outreach. Flexion and acetyl choline-like fluids serve that sequence, which is called Receiving Behavior.

Episodes of ambivalent interruption of the natural processes of coming (attachment) and going (separation) temporarily disrupt the smooth flow of the human animal's activity; but there is ordinarily rapid recovery of mind, body, soul, and physiology after such an episode. However because adult humans have the freedom to passively abdicate responsibility and initiative, the phenomenon of fixed *rôle-reversal* is possible. Parents with low self-esteem and those who are demoralized and embittered are inclined to establish a rôle-reversal between themselves and one or more of their children. In such a reversal the child is seduced into precocious privilege and responsibility, or simply forced for the sake of survival into taking on the parental role. The offending parent claims incapacity or inadequacy and requires that the child take care of her, at least psychologically and sometimes functionally as well. When a rôle-reversal is established the natural development of the child is interrupted and deranged, with far-reaching chronic patterns of dysfunction.

In healthy family circumstance, the parents spend most of their time and energy in a Providing mode whereas the children are predominantly in a Receiving mode. It is appropriate and necessary for the Provider to receive as well, mainly from the spouse and other adults but occasionally from the children. Similarly it is necessary for the Receiving children to extend into the environment, engaging in outreach activities, mainly with their friends and other children, but occasionally with their parents.

In the rôle-reversal these modes are reversed as well. The developing child then becomes burdened in mind and body, detached from his soul, and beset by age-inappropriate physiological flow. The parentified child is typically rigid or bent-over, hyperactive and interpersonally intrusive, mentally obsessional, and subject to the diseases of excessive adrenergic output (extensor dermatitis, migraine, hypertension, hyperthyroidism, benign cardiac arrhythmias, rheumatoid arthritis, and hemorrhoids). These are diseases of ambivalent Providing.

If the parent forces a rôle-exaggeration rather than reversal then the Parent locks into a pattern of excessive providing which induces the child into a passive receptivity. That child becomes clingingly dependent, sluggish in movement, slow-thinking, soul-bound with the parent, and subject to the diseases of excessive cholinergic flow (flexor dermatitis, hypothyroidism, peptic ulcer, diabetes, bronchial asthma, colitis, and diarrhea). These are diseases of ambivalent Receiving.

In rôle-reversal the self-discounting parent imputes grandeur to the subject child ("You are wonderful." "You are special." "I would die without you." "You can be anything you want to be"). If the child accepts the ascription of grandeur then he will incorporate that as grandiosity.

In rôle-exaggeration, the grandiose parent infantalizes the subject child, imputing to that child incapacity, inadequacy, insufficiency, and inferiority. ("Here, let me do that for you." "You're not old enough — strong enough — experienced enough — smart enough — to do that." "You always mess up." "I don't know what would become of you if I weren't around." "You've never had much ambition; you'll probably just stay here on the farm when you grow up.") If the child accepts the judgment of incapacity and helplessness then he will incorporate this as self-discounting.

The overvaluing by grandiosity and the undervaluing of discounting are recurring falsehoods (distortions) of the False Self System.

The naturally occurring affects of joy, sadness, anger, and fear are corrupted and exploited in the False Self System. All of the natural emotions are short-lived experiences appropriate to particular circumstance and episode but in the False Self System emotions are extended beyond any behavioral interaction which is unconsummated. So "bad feelings" linger, or persist, or even become fixed and characteristic.

If the human animal is mistreated or dealt with unfairly, he will respond with anger, which persists if there is no redress. The experience of repeated abuse leads to brooding unconsummated anger and ultimately to a fixed attitude of hostility.

The sadness of loss or disappointment calls in the natural order for comfort. If comforting is not supplied by the environmental parent the sadness will be unrelieved and will extend to "hurt feelings" and ultimately to depressive self-pity.

When a child is frightened, she needs to be held and reassured by protection and accurate information. In the absence of those healthy responses from the environment, the fear is extended to an anxious hypervigilance and ultimately to a readiness for panic or phobia.

Spontaneous joy, for its consummation, needs companionate celebration. That companion may be another person, a group of people, a domesticated animal (e.g. horse or dog), a human-friendly natural animal (dolphin), or a personified sense of Nature or of a creator. Joy which is not shared, not met by an environmental companion, is unbounded and escalates to a manic state which is not contactful. Repeated episodes of unshared joy lead to patterns of impulsive thrill-seeking and to episodes of explosive and gleeful "uncontrollable laughter" which is socially awkward and distancing. The manic distortion of natural joy is inevitably followed by depleted depression. Companionship is not possible in mania or depression because those states are non-contactible.

All these natural affects are simply the emotional components of the natural rhythmical behaviors of self-defense, of reparative grieving, of fear-allaying, and of celebration. There are other component behaviors which are simultaneously expressed in body movement (extension and/or flexion) and physiology (adrenergic and/or cholinergic flow). Natural affects are natural signals directing the human animal to emergency fight-or-flight behaviors, to refuge, or to companionate celebration. In the True Self System they are what they are, without value-judgments. In the False Self System those biological events are judged, labeled, and manipulated. They are generally referred to as "emotions" or "feelings." Particular families, sub-groups, and cultures attach varying values to specifically labeled emotions. All of those social clusters exercise Control by introducing and manipulating the un-natural pseudo-emotions of *guilt* and *shame*. Infants appear to experience the four natural affects but not guilt or shame.[7]

Guilt and shame are substitutions for natural affects which have not been consummated. They combine to "cover" unexpressed anger and sadness. The Controlling Parent teaches guilt as the proper response to "sins of commission" and shame as fitting for "sins of omission." Actually shame and guilt go hand-in-glove as the primers of "should" and "should not."

A child who has been manipulated by a self-discounting Parent into an assumption of grandiosity will divert most of his emotional energy into *guilty-anger*. He is angry at having to assume unrealistic responsibility and work overtime, and he feels guilty because his efforts at "fixing" other people and the world are never adequate.

The child who has been infantalized by a grandiose Parent will become self-discounting and experience an emotional compound of *shamed-sadness*. He is sad because he is not allowed growthful zest and ashamed because he can't "fix" himself.

The grandiose person is not allowed to experience sadness, so she is subject to depression. The discounted person is not allowed natural anger, but shaming provokes impotent rage which inclines her toward vengeful violence.

In these illustrations we have seen how the developing child is diverted into a False Self System with distortions of affect, mental functioning, anatomy, physiology, and social interaction (communication).

"Communication" in the False Self System is not only cognitively unclear, indirect, and incomplete but also it is injuriously used to express affects. Hurtful exaggerations and diminutions are inflicted by *sarcasm, facetiousness, teasing, irony, cynicism,* and *witty repartee*, all of which are animated by episodic anger or fixed hostility. "Cheerful" reminders are issued to off-set sadness and to substitute inadequately for comfort. Fear is frequently addressed by bravado or false reassurance. And joy is discouraged by cautionary predictions of come-down.

To this point in tracing the development of the False Self System, the focus has been mainly "dyadic"; that is, involving two principals only, (1) the developing Child and (2) the molding Parent or Parentified structure. I will now turn attention to the larger "triadic" world of Three: subject person, "the necessary other," and the Competitor.

Even in single-parent single-child family units there are implicit "third persons" or personifications: friends, enemies, lovers, cousins, peers, extended family members, male and female models (at school, in the neighborhood, in books or on television). All of these "third persons" are invoked for odious comparison, in competitive preference, or as idealized models.

In the more typical family unit with at least two adults and several children, the competition is constant and consequential. The parents compete subtly or openly "to be the better parent" and each child strives to be seen as "the best child." Furthermore there are various alliances of pairs or clusters. Paired alliances exist, for example, between one child and one of the parents; clustered alliances are represented, for instance, by "all the girls."

The general formula for the "family triangle" is "I-you-the other/others." The most publicized triangle involves the Oedipal conflict described by Sigmund Freud. According to that perspective, every child at some point in early development, at least, craves a preferential relationship with the parent of the opposite sex. The desired ownership cannot be consummated, and the vicissitudes of the Oedipal conflict do indeed color for life the subject's basic relationship to both women and men. Ideally for the developing child there would be two resident parents who would each relate empathically to the child's yearnings, competitive death-wishes, and disappointments. That ideal is rarely realized and most children experience the original three-person struggle as trauma and drama.

For the human animal life is dramatized by any interference, interruption, suspension, deferment, or non-consummation of a natural sequence. The two basic distortions which dramatize the Oedipal conflict are *overstimulation* and *ruthless suppression.* A developing child (and the later adult) is damaged by an unrealistic "Yes" or by a harsh and punitive "No!" That truism applies not only to the issues of Oedipal striving, but to *all* wishes that the child expresses.

Non-sustainable promise and *punitive rejection* both serve to dramatize the child's life, initially in the interpersonal environment and eventually inside the psychic structure (Ego-container) of that child.

One of the "second-generation" contributors to the theories of Transactional Analysis, Stephen Karpman, devised a very simple and very useful model of dramatization. [8] Karpman's Drama Triangle features three roles or positions or players: *Persecutor, Victim,* and *Rescuer.* One can "enter" the triangle at any one of the three positions, ordinarily prompted by some current life-circumstance. The human animal can "stage" the drama privately or publicly or, as is most often the case, partly internal and partly projected into the interpersonal world. For instance, one might be "victimized" in the objective world by being passed over for promotion, whereupon one acts out a subjective "rescue" with an extravagant shopping spree. Or one might gratuitously intervene in an observed interaction between two contending people, one appearing to be a Persecutor and the other a Victim. The observer steps in as Rescuer and shortly becomes the Victim, "persecuted" perhaps by both of the former antagonists who seize the opportunity for pseudo-equal alliance.

One of the clearest and most crucial distinctions between the False Self System and the True Self System rests on the contrast between the drama of the False and the matter-of-fact ordinariness of the True. Responsibility to oneself and empathic appropriate responsiveness to the environments (personal and natural) provide liveliness, excitement, creativity, wonder, delight, full affective engagement, and spontaneity — but not drama. Drama requires suspended animation, mysteriousness (as contrasted with healthy acceptance of mystery), and a focus on motive.

Given the fact that all human animals are raised in False Self Systems, of varying rigor, it follows that every person spends time in the subjective world of dramatic interpretation. Some people spend most of their life's time in the Drama Triangle.

The script (see Chapter 2) is a dramatic life-plan conceived in the nuclear family as an unnatural replacement for the unfolding ground plan ("instructions") of the nuclear Self. The Drama Triangle is the dynamic motor of the script. Children/persons emerge from the family matrix with a clearly assigned "lead role" as Rescuer (helper, healer, peace-maker), Persecutor (boss, judge, watchdog, monitor, fixer), or Victim (sacrificer, self-denier, acquiescer, absorber). The person can consciously identify that role, usually in one of its "virtuous" forms, and other family members (and the general public) concur with that role-assumption. The person ordinarily believes that he chose the role consciously. He is usually not aware of the behavioral and attitudinal patterns that recurrently "land" him in his major role, and he is generally oblivious to the sequential occupancy of his two minor position-roles.

The script is written and directed by the child's parents, with modifications introduced by members of the extended family and by fate (unusual gifts of beauty, brightness, or stature; or unusual liabilities of ugliness, dullness, or physical deformity.) For their own restitutional or vengeful purposes parents single out children to follow dramatic scripts which have either tragic or glorious outcomes. The activity of the Drama Triangle serves, as it were, to keep the person busy until the denouement of the script.

In the True Self System other people are contacted for reciprocal enrichment. Realistic appraisal, adequate experimentation, and thoughtful discrimination lead to selection of "other persons" (friends, mates, colleagues) who are interdependent equals, sharing common values and interests.

In the False Self System other people are "contracted" (not contacted) to serve as cast-members for one's script. The contract is based on recognizable inequality and co-dependence. Love-at-first-sight, fascination, or fatal attraction lead to uncanny selection of persons who will fill the minor complements to one's own major role. So Victims unerringly select Persecutors and vice versa. The programmed Rescuer has slightly greater latitude, being able to select either a Victim to revive and restore or a Persecutor to reform.

The unprogrammed exchanges between persons in the True Self System (an open system) provide balanced nutrition, steady-state energy, and mutual growth. The regulated homeostatic ("keep the peace"; "eliminate error") exchanges of the False Self System (a closed system) move toward entropy, toward mutual depletion of energy, interest, and morale. New energy in that system is periodically infused by "cannibalizing" fresh players enlisted from one's captive audience.

Most people literally "kill" time while awaiting the dramatic denouement of their unconsciously programmed life-scripts. The ordained outcome is either glory (One's ship coming in!) or tragedy (One's ship sinking!). Before the "final scene of the final act" there are periodic approximations to "arrival" or "ruin." Between these episodes of almost-consummation of the script, many people use their time and energy autonomously enjoying life under True Self direction, and participating usefully in the common culture. The pattern of recurring almost-consummations of the script is that same pattern designated as the "repetition-compulsion" by psychoanalysis and recognized in mythology as Fate or Destiny.

The human animal, reared in the False Self System, is under compulsion to repeat because she was compelled in the early years to accept the assigned role as a condition of dependent support.

"Waiting" is a prominent behavior in the False Self System. That waiting is passive and impatient. It is generally rationalized, either in grandiose terms ("I'm waiting for the right time.") or in discounting terms ("Well, I'm just a procrastinator like my daddy was. Ha! Ha!"). The magical thinking which informs the dramatic life "in the script" believes that the glorious denouement can be brought about by sufficient rapturous anticipation ("Wishing will make it so!"), or that the tragic denouement can be forestalled by dread ("If I worry about it enough, it won't happen.")

Recall that the script is composed of counter-natural messages from the parental structure to the developing child. All the children in a family might receive some of these script-messages in common but each child will also get specific "instructions" for fulfilling a particular role. The messages are

called injunctions (Don't . . .) and counterinjunction or drivers
(Do . . .) A child selected to be a heroic caretaker might be given
these assignments: Don't Be a Child, Don't Be Emotional, Don't
Be Selfish; and Be Brilliant, Be Strong, Be Cheerful, Persevere,
Try Hard. Or a child who is a designated scapegoat and serves
as a perpetual excuse for an infantalizing parent has been
instructed: Don't Grow Up, Don't Venture, Don't Fight, Be
Sickly, Complain and Whine, Be Pitiful, for instance. Some
unwanted children oblige the parent-person by "accidental"
death or suicide.

The child accepts the False Self System with its script
and drama triangle and guilt and shame and designated
rôle only because of obligatory dependent needs. The
child invariably arranges a compromise with the parental
structure in such a way as to maximize the supply of dependent needs and to minimize the damage done by surrender
of initiative.

In a subsequent chapter the derivative benefits of
"secondary gain" within the compromise will be detailed. For
now I need to introduce the concept of secondary-gain as
framework for "the secret life."

All cultures apparently develop myths and fairy-tales which
are passed on through successive generations in written form
or by story-telling. Myths announce the fate and destiny of
human beings imposed by deities or gods. Fairy-tales provide
escapes from those fateful sentences and curses issued by the
gods, or witches, or giants. The common "family" perspective
characteristic of fairy-tales is transparent, whereas the context
of the mythical stories is, like the script, less obvious. In Western
society children and adults much more readily identify with
Cinderella or Jack the Giant-Killer than with Sisyphus or
Narcissus.

Presumably every person indulges private fantasies which, like fairy-tales, have wish-fulfilling outcomes or dreaded conclusions. Most of the fantasy content involves romance (the ideal sexual relationship), victorious combat (overthrow of the bad guy), or the achievement of fame or fortune (winning the Nobel Prize or finding the pot of gold). These fantasies do provide temporary escape from one's disappointed life and they actually deliver some short-lived gratification. As is true with activity in the Drama Triangle, one's "secret life" can be entirely private or acted-out with other players. Embezzlement, illicit sexual activity and heroic rescue are common enactments "planned" in secret chambers.

Upon inquiry people promptly recall "funeral fantasies" from childhood as well as in later life. Those fantasies range from the whimpering pay-off of "They'll be sorry" or "Finally they'll understand" to the elaborate celebration authored by Winston Churchill for his last hurrah.

Within the imaginings of the secret life people have secret identities and sometimes even secret names. James Thurber's character Walter Mitty was a creative fountain of heroic identities. The secret identity most often provides alternatives to the determinism of the script and of the role-assignment. At some level of dim consciousness every person recognizes that she or he is being short-changed and under-appreciated; there is also hazy recognition of collusive participation in the artificial script. Out of those vapors arise common secret identities as either "undiscovered genius" ("Sometimes I think I really am smart.") or "unexposed impostor" ("I often feel like a phoney").

All human beings are abused and victimized, especially in the vulnerable years of childhood. Not getting what they deserve and being dealt with arbitrarily and unfairly, children decide that they are ENTITLED. The sense of entitlement is one of the most pernicious features of the False Self System. Victimized children and adults take law and justice into their own heads and hands. They do secret book-keeping and score-keeping, decide on arbitrary quid pro quo compensation, and confer upon themselves various immunities from ordinary citizenship.

Children traumatized by parental divorce frequently invoke secret entitlement which allows them to steal, without a sense of guilt or remorse. Persons who are sexually frustrated in their marriages commonly claim entitlement to an extra-marital affair, preferably with another married person! Oppressed groups in society often claim entitlement to special consideration and they confer self-immunity from ordinary requirements.

Eric Berne's theoretical system, Transactional Analysis, describes the elements of the script and shows how those elements are sequentially related. [9] In the same sense that there is a "favorite" major role in the Drama Triangle, each person also has a favorite "bad feeling" which corresponds to the major role. Berne calls these bad feeling states "rackets" because of the inevitably manipulative way they are used on the interpersonal environment. Again there is a compromise-formation in which the person is willing to feel bad (depressed, angry, jealous, anxious, paranoid, etc.) in order to extort certain benefits from other people.

Berne observed a particular kind of secret scorekeeping which he called "stamp collecting." His model followed the format of collecting mercantile stamps to be traded in for a prize when a particular number of stamps was accumulated. He proposed that in these private schemes, people declared their own prize (theft, inebriation, divorce, an affair, early retirement, physical illness) after a magically-determined number of victimizations. Gratuitously-arranged episodes were sometimes sought to complete the collection or to add the "last straw."

"Game-playing," as defined by Berne, involved a series of collusionary interactions with a predictable outcome in "bad feelings" and in reinforcing one's role-position and script outcome. Interpersonal "games" are sophisticated almost-consummated engagements which provide close approach with guaranteed avoidance of intimacy. Domestic civility and international diplomacy, both high-level games, are devoted to peace but not to justice. The interpersonal pathology described in Berne's system of Transactional Analysis is an apt paraphrase of the False Self System.

False Self Systems are "narcissistic" systems, in the pejorative sense of that word. In my theoretical constructions, that translates into "systems with weak Ego-containers." Recall that in an earlier section I proposed that the narcissistic energy of the Self is amoral and that it "wants" nothing from the environment other than recognition and attention.

The True Self System is built on truth, accuracy, statistical probability, candor, scientific causality, and realism. Those commodities are the characteristics and the sustenances of a strong, flexible, reliable Ego-container. A strong Ego closely monitors what comes in and what goes out across the limiting membrane.

The False Self System built as it is on pretense, denial, magic, hope, and unreality is weak, rigid, leaky, and therefore unreliable. The weak container does not guard its own boundaries well from either direction, allowing toxic intake and failing to regulate the outflow of narcissistic energy. Accordingly life in the False Self System is characterized by attention-gaining behaviors. The grandiose-exhibitionistic behaviors of normal early childhood are not ripened into healthy ambition and creativity but are continued into adult life as arrogant boasting or as imperious self-pity. In a word, life in the False Self System is highly exhibitionistic. Those who flaunt and those who pout are both unbalanced and are both unavailable for reciprocally nourishing contact.

Addiction to anesthetizing substances, behaviors, and relationships are prominent alternatives in the False Self System. Neither the "self-sufficient" Dominator nor the self-denying Submitter is inclined to ask directly for ordinary nourishment; to do that would violate and jeopardize the fixed rôle. Refusing ordinary natural nutriments (affection, comfort, soothing, quiet presence, and physical touch), the human animal in the False Self System is subject to indulging extraordinary un-natural appetites. Conspicuous consumption, insatiable and wasteful, is characteristic of individuals and collectives in the False Self System. Overeating and obesity, over-imbibing and alcoholism, money-making and money-spending, empire-building and proprietary expansion, and collecting and acquiring are all quantitative addictions. Drugs which alter mood and mind, vehicular speeding, gambling, sexual athleticism, warfare between gangs and nations, sado-masochistic energy transfers, and religious transport illustrate more qualitative deviations from the reciprocal enrichment provided in the worlds of nature and people.

The dependent adapting child must submit to the parental establishment, but the child learns to compromise for maximum gain (gratification) and minimum loss (frustration and injury). In paraphrase the human animal seeks pleasure and avoids pain. Addictions provide transient pleasure and they anesthetize against pain. Short of addiction is the related phenomenon of habituation which can provide familiar predictable comfort, without the obvious dangers of addictive behaviors. "Training" is a term common to the vocabularies of child-rearing, physical capacity, and the development of skills generally. Training allows behavior which is increasingly automatic, decision-free, unreflective, and therefore energy saving. Human behavior is entrained in psychomotor sequences which involve the elements of stimulus, perception, assessment, and response. Like a railway train, a habituated sequence is linear, hooked together, and grooved on a neuronal track.

A child learns the rules, the amenities, and the manners of family and sub-group and then habituates the prescribed responses to repetitive stimulus-cues from the environment. There is pain in submitting to unrelenting requirements, in having to "always remember." There is pleasure in being approved and accepted, in belonging. There is pleasure in claiming superiority over the less-mannerly. There is pain in recognizing one's self-righteousness. And there is painful discomfort in observing the mechanical emptiness of rote training, of insincerity, of "going through the motions." This combination of pains and pleasures illustrates the compromise-formation inevitable to socialization.

What trained habituation gains in the conservation of energy and in the cloning of civility, it loses in spontaneity, contactfulness, novelty, and enrichment. Well-trained children who become well-trained adults frequently fail to understand why behaviors which pleased their parents alienate and distance their contemporaries. The compromise combinations of pleasure and pain continue and expand in the False Self Systems.

As the human animal matures and moves from an obligatory dependency which required painful submission there is an inclination to seek pleasure only and to avoid pain entirely. In and out of therapy people commonly seek "happiness" (perpetual pleasure) and they wish to "get rid of" pain and discomfort (anxiety, sadness, anger, guilt, shame).

One day in her therapy group Rosalie announced, "I want to give up my anger." I asked how she planned to do that and how we could be of help. She responded that she was going to watch herself more closely and use her will-power to hold it in. She wanted us to "support" her in doing that. I did not point out the ironic contradiction lodged in the intention to "give up" her anger by holding it in! I simply observed silently how faithful that double-bind formula is to the instructions of the False Self System.

I asked Rosalie what benefits her anger brought her. She retorted quickly, "It doesn't bring me anything but trouble. When people mistreat me, I don't show my anger at first, then I brood about the mistreatment, then I explode at someone who wasn't even involved. Then I feel guilty."

I repeated, "See if you can identify some benefits in that pattern." Rosalie became reflective for a moment, then her face brightened. "Well, it's familiar; I've been doing that all my life." Next she smiled slightly and said, "Yeah, and it's peculiar but I feel powerful when I explode and I also feel powerful getting ready to explode. Yeah, and while I'm brooding I enjoy imagining torturing my enemies." At that she laughed and was joined by identifying laughter around the room. Now, on something of a roll, Rosalie continued, "I just realized too that I usually explode at someone who'll be understanding and will forgive me. It feels good to be forgiven. I guess I feel forgiven then for not standing up to the people who hurt me." Suddenly her face fell and Rosalie cried vacantly for a moment. She looked up and said, "When I mentioned people who hurt me I thought way back to childhood when my Daddy would be mean to Mother. Mother did just the way I do - she clammed up, then brooded, then exploded at me and later said how sorry she was that she'd done that. We'd usually hug each other and cry. I felt very close to her at those times." Another pause, then, "It's strange but it feels good to cry. I hardly ever cry or feel sad anymore, I thought if I felt sad it would be like giving-up. Does my anger protect me from sadness?"

In brief compass Rosalie has identified the multiple interlocking benefits of her False System, of which the undesirable "anger" is but the tip of the iceberg. Without using my technical jargon she has cited role-reversal, passivity, indirectness, displacement, movements around the Drama Triangle, manipulation by affect, co-dependency, and habituation, among others.

The False Self System is like Ezekiel's Valley of the Dry Bones. And like Ezekiel's rebuilt person it comes to life through the infusion of affect, but affect which is stolen from the child and misappropriated. All the bones are connected to the next bones, but they're old bones, family bones.

Affect (emotion) is the basic energy of life for the human animal. In the False Self System affect is abused and used manipulatively to extort benefits and to establish control over other persons. In that system the natural healthy affects are disallowed or diverted or amplified, but not honored.

In the natural healthy True System children are allowed to be sad at disappointment and loss. They are contained comfortably and allowed to cry until they decide they've cried enough. Similarly anger, and joy, and fear are allowed to run their circumstantial courses with disinterested empathic containment. In that system the child's affect is neither "fixed" nor vicariously appropriated by the parent. All feelings are honored as are body parts and personal idiosyncracies. In that system everything is sacred and nothing is a big deal. In the dramatic False Self System, by contrast, everything is a big deal and nothing is authentically sacred.

Corrupted affect is the fuel for the False Self System. That corruption is a many-splintered thing:

(1) Affect is an index for quality of life in the False Self System. "Happiness" is widely accepted as the sine qua non of the "good life." A story attributed to Elie Wiesel gives lie to that association.

"A young man comes running to his home at mid-day shouting to his mother to break out the champagne, that his promotion has just been announced. The rapturous mother meets him at the door; they embrace with joyful tearful celebration. She stands back, holds him proudly with her eyes and murmurs, "I can't believe it — my own son — the commander of Auschwitz!"" That their happiness and joy was real is not arguable, but what of the context?

In a parallel corruption, sadness is suspect in the False System. It frequently evokes the old "bad" question, "What's the matter with you?"

(2) Affect is misappropriated as a latter-day transitional object (like the toddler's blanket or teddy-bear which symbolically connects to the parents). In the anecdote above about Rosalie we see an example of that adult woman reconnecting to the childhood mother through her habituated affective sequence.

A country-western ballad lampoons this phenomenon with the title, "I'm So Miserable Here Without You, It's Almost Like You Were Here."

(3) Affective displacement and diffusion is a compromise-settlement when specific affects are disallowed or dishonored. So adult humans who have not been allowed focused affect consummated with appropriate response (e.g. fear met by reassurance; sadness met with comfort) must settle for what they and others call "emotionality" or "sentimentality." These panoramic, and non-specific emotional reactions are not contactible, satisfying, or enriching.

This dissection (analysis) of the False Self System has been like the dissection of other dead bodies (from frogs to cadavers): tedious, surprising, awesome, fearful, complex, and systematic. Like the others, it is also a necessary discipline for the greater appreciation of biology, biography, and life. It is also a necessary preparation for healing, recovery, and therapy.

Chapter 13

Secondary Gain And
The Logic Of Survival

FOR ALL THE ANIMALS *SURVIVAL* IS ALWAYS THE TOP PRIORITY. In order to save its life animals, including the human animal, will surrender or sacrifice a function or a body part if the controlling restraining environment requires that surrender. Four-legged animals caught by the leg in a steel trap have been known to gnaw the limb off in order to escape. Human animals similarly surrender or curtail or hide intelligence, beauty, creativity, skill or independent thought in order to "get along with" parents or siblings or groups who are threatened by the expression of those natural functions. Such is the logic of survival.

"Secondary gain" is a term from the general field of medicine recognizing people's ability to derive some benefit or "gain" from sickness, injury, or loss. This is the clinical version of making purses out of sows' ears.

One of the common and relatively benign recognitions of secondary gain occurs when someone says, "I felt lousy for a couple of days, but then I was glad I had the flu. It was a good excuse to stay home."

An even more common but less benign and little recognized pattern of secondary gain is acknowledged by one of the speakers in W. H. Auden's "The Age of Anxiety." Auden has observed:

> "... it is silly to refuse the tasks of time and, overlooking our
> lives, cry
> 'Miserable, wicked me! How interesting I am.'
> We would rather be ruined than changed
> We would rather die in our dread
> Than climb the cross of the moment
> And let our illusions die." [10]

The implication that people *prefer* to be ruined rather than changed or to die in dread rather than confront a challenging task sounds perverse. But measured by the logic of survival, it "makes sense" to guard one's familiar misery rather than to venture into the promising unknown. And it "makes sense" to discount oneself ("Miserable, wicked me . . .") if doing that will forestall any discounting or competitive striving by one's rivals.

Children take on special rôles in the family of origin. Sometimes the rôles are explicitly assigned by parents, sometimes they are required by circumstance (as in the death or disability of a parent), and sometimes the child apparently chooses a rôle idiosyncratically. Whatever the designated rôle it will almost certainly be overemphasized, overpracticed, and overdone to the exclusion of other natural functions and behaviors.

Fred was a child appointed to keep the family cheerful. He dutifully became a perpetual Clown. In adult life he observes that he has difficulty being serious in serious circumstance. He also observes that other people do not take him seriously. His wife who was initially attracted by his cheerfulness now complains about his boyish clowning and tells him that she has lost respect for him. In spite of the fact that he is bright, conscientious, and has good work habits he has been repeatedly passed over for promotion in his company because of the clowning. In his marriage and in his job, the rôle assigned Fred when he was a child is seriously problematic, but Fred doesn't change. He briefly reforms, by promise and will-power, but quickly he becomes anxious and depressed without his habitual behavior, to which he then returns.

I do not believe that Fred can substantially change unless he understands the illusion behind his behavior and the power of that illusion. I don't know how Fred or any other person can discover that except in psychotherapy. The basic illusion which drives Fred's behavior and which confers overriding secondary gain is the unconscious belief that if he clowns long enough and well enough he can protect his long-dead mother from depression and that he will accordingly be acclaimed and loved by everyone! This is the magnitude of the illusions which Auden recognizes we are reluctant to let die.

It is striking to observe how readily people in psychotherapy can identify the benefits (the secondary gain) of "problems" when asked. Recall the illustration of Rosalie in Chapter 12, (page 105) where she quickly ticks off the sequence of benefits which her injurious angry behavior pattern provides her.

Foremost among the benefits of "wicked misery" are familiarity, notoriety, attention-getting, immunity from the challenge of new behavior, psychological attachment to childhood and to one's parents, protection from ordinariness, conservation of energy by using habituated reflexes, and maintenance of the central illusions.

The self-interest reflected in Auden's claim, "How interesting I am" is recognizable in the hypochondriac who is fascinated by the details of his own ill-health. It is the Narcissus in us which gazes fondly in the mirror of our misery (brief or sustained), indulging first self-pity and soon self-righteousness.

While fascinating oneself with a recitation of ills and victimizations, one draws a crowd of fellow-sufferers and bores healthy people to the point of departure. On the balance of secondary gain, it's worth it!

Self-righteousness is one of the mainstays of secondary gain and one of the mechanisms for the survival of self-esteem. A Swiss colleague of mine told me about a patient of his who was a self-righteous potato-hater. In his childhood Stefan responded to his perfectionistic mother's rigid insistence on "healthy food only" by overeating and becoming a fat-boy, to the mother's expressed disgust. His favorite food was mashed potatoes and he frequently "made himself sick" overindulging. Stefan's mother made dire predictions about his bleak future — "you will lose all your teeth if you keep eating potatoes" and "no one will like you if you're fat." Eventually Stefan incorporated his mother's disgust. He not only gave up eating potatoes but he became scornful of all potato-eaters. He consulted my colleague for treatment of his long-time depression. During the first session Stefan told the therapist that the only thing that made him feel good was counting the potato-eaters in Geneva! He had developed the compulsive habit of walking the streets twice each day and counting the people in open-air and windowed restaurants who were eating potatoes. He kept meticulous records of his sightings. "On a good day," he told my colleague, "I might spot over three-hundred." That would translate into three-hundred increments of elevated self-esteem and three-hundred anonymous scornful citations.

The childhood survival decisions which are parlayed into secondary gain share in common with those of the Potato Hater a compromise trade-off. Essentially the compromised and compromising child accepts deprivation and humiliation in exchange for self-righteousness, self-indulgence, immunity, and other unhealthy narcissistic invocations. It is also typical that the benefits in secondary gain are themselves problematic. For the Potato Counter there was an enormous expenditure of time and energy required to maintain his drug-like habit. Inevitably the pay-offs of secondary gain are socially dysfunctional because of their self-serving nature.

Short of self-destruction, the most extreme application of the "survival-secondary gain compromise" is what is known diagnostically as "Self-Defeating Personality Disorder." In the American Psychiatric Association's current manual (DSM-III-R) [11] the criteria for this clinical label are listed:

A. A pervasive pattern of self-defeating behavior, beginning by early adulthood and present in a variety of contexts. The person may often avoid or undermine pleasurable experiences, be drawn to situations or relationships in which he or she will suffer, and prevent others from helping him or her, as indicated by at least five of the following:

(1)   chooses people and situations that lead to disappointment, failure, or mistreatment even when better options are clearly available

(2)   rejects or renders ineffective the attempts of others to help him or her

(3)   following positive personal events (e.g., new achievement), responds with depression, guilt or a behavior that produces pain (e.g., an accident)

(4)   incites angry or rejecting responses from others and then feels hurt, defeated, or humiliated (e.g., makes fun of spouse in public, provoking an angry retort, then feels devastated)

(5)   rejects opportunities for pleasure, or is reluctant to acknowledge enjoying himself or herself (despite having adequate social skills and the capacity for pleasure)

(6)   fails to accomplish tasks crucial to his or her personal objectives despite demonstrated ability to do so, e.g., helps fellow students write papers, but is unable to write his or her own

(7)   is uninterested in or rejects people who consistently treat him or her well, i.e., is unattracted to caring sexual partners

(8)   engages in excessive self-sacrifice that is unsolicited by the intended recipients of the sacrifice

I am convinced that all human beings, unhealthy and healthy as well, will return under stress to ancient survival patterns including self-defeating behavior. We will do what we have to in order to survive.

Unhealthy secondary gain stands in contrast to the human animal's healthy capacity for *substitution* and *compensation*. Some children afflicted in the polio epidemics learned to make the unwithered arm "as strong as two arms." Such courageous recovery hardly ever promotes self-sighteousness, but rather quiet pride and gratitude.

Chapter 14

BONNIE: RETURN TO THE ORDINARY

P ERHAPS EVEN IN UTERO BONNIE WAS INJURED BY THE rancor and recriminations between her parents when they learned she was on the way.

Ella was forty-two when Bonnie was conceived. She was menopausal and unconcerned that the infrequent and perfunctory intercourse with Bryan would issue in pregnancy. Ella assumed that her husband would not want another child so she kept her secret until the fourth month, having decided to her surprise that she very much wanted another baby. Of the three earlier children Kevin and Mark were away in college and Kathleen was a high school senior living at home. The family was well-heeled financially, secured by Bryan's business success and Ella's inheritance. But the long-standing civil animosity between Ella and Bryan had taken its toll and all five of the family members lived somewhere between subdued and depressed.

Bryan, in keeping with Ella's predictions, reacted to the news with alarm and accusations of his wife's irresponsibility. "What do you mean you forgot your diaphragm? Jesus Christ, Ella! Do you realize what this will do to our lives?" Ella had also predicted privately that Bryan's doctrinaire Catholicism would safeguard her pregnancy. She was correct in that assumption.

So Bryan seethed quietly through the last trimesters, alternately cursing his wife and the Pope.

Mark and Kevin were slightly embarrassed, but largely non-committal. Kathleen, on the other hand, was overjoyed and she became her mother's happy handmaiden as the two of them decorated the nursery and waited with excitement.

Ella blossomed with her manifestation. She thoroughly enjoyed the amused envy of her country-club cronies and she delighted in the sudden companionship with Kathleen and with Kathleen's friends.

Buoyed by such unaccustomed support, Ella noticed a quickening of her own spirit and a resumption of long-lost warmth and charity. She had learned through the years of her marriage to live around the edges of Bryan's hostile demoralization and to settle into a dutiful resignation. But now in her last trimester she watched herself watching Bryan and initially distrusting the sympathetic and appreciative feelings of warmth toward him. She thought that his brooding was shifting to a softer reflectiveness, and again her intuition was correct. Ella chose the moment carefully to say to Bryan in as matter-of-fact a voice as she could muster, "Bryan, if our baby is a boy I want him named for your Dad and if it's a girl let's name her for that good woman Bonnie."

During the recent months Bryan had noticed the shifts in his home environment. He was startled to realize that he was looking forward to "coming home" as he drove from work. Earlier in the year his approaching fiftieth birthday had loomed like an albatross but now he laughed to hear the jingle in his head, "Father at Fifty! Father at Fifty!"

When Ella proposed the naming of the child to Bryan, he was taken off-guard. The uneasy and unaccustomed peace was fragile. The private warming inside the two ancient enemies was still secret, waiting for a sign.

Moved by his wife's uncluttered offering Bryan initially took refuge in the negative. "I couldn't name a boy for my father yet. I still haven't forgiven him for the way he treated Mother." He paused and looked straight into Ella's face through his tears. Choking, he awkwardly reached for Ella and hugged her. "Thank you, Ella." Their hard-line linear bodies gradually rounded and held.

Several night later Ella and Bryan were lying abed wearing the vacant grins of newly-weds and marveling together about their reconciliation. They wondered aloud how it happened. After Ella murmured, "Bryan, I really don't think it's because I'm going to have a baby. What feels so different is having all those people loving me so much while I'm pregnant. And the real miracle is that you love me again."

Bryan turned quiet and thoughtful. Then, "I can't explain what has happened to me. I was so depressed about life generally, about college tuitions, about turning fifty, about our relationship. When you told me you were pregnant I thought for several days about how to kill myself and have it look like an accident. Then out of the blue Hal Pusey walked into my office and handed me a poem. I didn't know Hal read anything, let alone poetry. Anyway it's by a guy named Carl Dennis — I'd never heard of him but I think he and Hal saved my life. I made a copy. I'd like for you to read it."

Ella wiped her tears and said simply, "I'd like to." Bryan fished out a single sheet from the briefcase on his bedroom study-table. His hand and the paper trembled when he handed it to Ella. "Here it is."

Ella read, transfixed:

On My Fiftieth Birthday

Now I'm as old as my father was
When less than a year was left him.
His good deeds couldn't lengthen his life by a day.
What's left of them now, after thirty years,
But ghostly images?

Last night in my birthday dream,
Coming home to a house sunk in the ground
Past the first floor window,
I found him sitting alone
In the unlit foyer, his head in his hands.

Something he'd left undone still worried him
When he should have been looking down
On the past from a restful star
Where the just dwell, looking down
On an earth grown small and make-believe.

Instead, he was stuck in a dark foyer
Grieving, it seemed to me, though we didn't speak,
That he'd left me his doubtful habits,
Not the ones he trusted,
That he'd failed to put the pain of his youth
Behind him before he married.

He must have assumed that the book of his life
Was closed when his life closed.
Now, because of me, it lay open,
Open to amendment, and not the last page only
But the early ones as well, the rebuffs

His mother received as a girl,
The dreary summers his father spent as a boy
At the stodgy resort where he had no companions.

Whole chapters of his life have been blown away
And lost, not carved on the stone walls
Of a tomb chapel to shame the death gods.
And still his case isn't closed.
The evidence is still being gathered.
What happens now finds room in the margins
That seemed before too crowded for addenda. [12]

Bryan became tearful watching Ella's appreciative tears interrupt her reading. She finished and quietly gathered Bryan to her swollen breasts. "Thank God for Carl Dennis! How can someone know that much about life?"

They were both peacefully silent for a long time. Then Bryan spoke with cautious wonderment. "I don't know whether Dennis intended it or knew about it or even whether it's true, but I realized that the poem is about life — I mean, an individual's life, not just about the generations. In that last verse, I changed "his" to "my" and I know that's true. I don't know if I really believe in angels or divine intervention or stuff like that, but how can I explain an unlikely poem-reader friend bringing me a poem by somebody I'd never heard of? It looks like a different world out there if I remember the Dennises and the Puseys. And I think I'm beginning to forgive my father."

Bryan and Ella O'Rourke came to consult with me almost thirty years ago shortly after Bonnie's first birthday. Their relationship was close and nurturant and they were both perplexed by their sudden downturn. The previous year, they said,

"Was the best year either of us ever had." Everything about Bonnie's arrival had gone well; the labor was easy; Bonnie was healthy and beautiful, and when Bryan held the newborn Bonnie it was bonding at first sight. When Bonnie was a month old, Ella who was still on a roll arranged a mammoth fiftieth birthday celebration for an appreciative Bryan. A few months after that Ella and Bryan began to notice changes in themselves and in the other — similar symptoms of restlessness, anxiety, fleeting depression and increasing consumption of alcohol.

They came quickly for help, confessing that they had turned briefly in desperation to popular self-help articles on menopause, post-partum depression, and mid-life crisis. "We knew better," Bryan apologized, "but we were both confused. It was hard to believe that we were having problems when everything had gotten so good. I thought that maybe we just couldn't stand prosperity."

I saw Ella and Bryan, jointly and separately, for less than four months and they were on their way again, a bit shakily but confident.

Bryan's off-handed comment about not being able to stand prosperity was diagnostic.

"Prosperity" is hard to take for a number of reasons. Of the various prosperities financial wealth is probably the easiest to tolerate, especially in an affluent society. But the sudden prosperity of widespread support and friendship is quite literally hard to digest and to assimilate. And surely the most unaccustomed prosperity, that of intimate relationship, requires a reordering of expectations, defenses, and attitudes.

There is a truism about personal support which defies the common logic; namely, human beings need far more support when things are freshly going well than when life is stressful or miserable.

After the communal celebration of Ella's near-miraculous conception and after the outpouring of comradeship for Bryan's Fiftieth, the support began to fall away. Bryan and Ella had neither the awareness, nor the boldness, nor the training to call back the fading support. Much co-celebration of life events comes from identification and is therefore vicarious. That's all right as far as it goes, but it simply doesn't go very far. Vicarious participation is often tinged with envy and is generally devoid of empathy. The human animal needs constant empathic support which is sustainable in bad times and good, in the extraordinary and especially in the ordinary.

My work with the two O'Rourkes was pleasant, inspiring, enriching, and fun. I enjoyed hearing the story they told me. My therapeutic task was the simplest one — explanation and demystification. I did have the mildly stressful assignment of helping these two good reformed brooders re-mobilize their healthy anger and their legitimate disappointment in the fair-weather friends.

Bonnie O'Rourke Ellis telephoned recently to certify that I was "still in practice" and to ask for an appointment.

I had never met Bonnie but I felt like I knew her aforehand. I knew that she was born into extraordinary circumstance, that her conception and birth had occasioned extraordinary recovery of a family, and I recognized as extraordinary the fact that I was to see the child of former patients. At least I knew to counter my positive countertransference with vigilance.

Bonnie arrived, overflowing my full-glass expectations. She was beautiful, well-proportioned of face and figure, poised, warm, and very bright. She made my work no easier with her greeting, "I've heard about you all my life. My folks think you're wonderful." I replied, "Thank you." After many years of trial-and-error I have learned that when I am doing psychotherapy I cannot ward off either grandiose or discounting evaluations. I can however let them die natural deaths if I do not argue with them or reply in kind (e.g. "You're wonderful too.").

That awkwardness survived, Bonnie and I sat studying each other, both with practiced correctness. I asked, "What do you want and how can I be of help?" Bonnie grinned and chortled, "That's exactly what Mom said you'd ask me." I neither grinned nor frowned and Bonnie sobered. Slowly her face fell and she became tearful in a way that did not contradict the genuineness of her earlier light-hearted warmth.

"I'm in a mess. My marriage is a mess. My child is a mess. And I don't understand what has happened. I thought I had the world on a string until two or three years ago. You probably know that I'm a family therapist (I didn't). In 1991 I was appointed director of the family therapy section in the state system — it seems that's when things began to go downhill. My husband — his name is Jack — started criticizing me and carping at me. He'd never done that before and I began imagining that he was having an affair. I asked him if he was. He just exploded and he yelled at me, 'That's just like you — always locating the problem outside yourself. You're the most self-centered spoiled person I've ever known.' Then he ran around the house yanking down all my framed certificates and some beauty pageant pictures of me — and he was the one who had put them up in the first place — over my objections. I did think that Jack had the problem and was taking it out on me. But then one day at the office I was in the toilet stall and two of my friends came into the bathroom. They were talking about me and one of them said, 'I like Bonnie but I'd hate to live with her. She's everybody's darling and she's spoiled rotten. I bet she throws her underwear on the floor.' I just sat real still in my stall, feeling shocked and kind of dizzy. Finally they left. I thought I was going to throw up. I was flooded with memories of my parents and my sister saying I was spoiled rotten, but they always laughed when they said it. And worse than that I saw myself tearing into Jane — she's our six year old daughter — and telling her she's a spoiled brat when she asks for anything extra. I feel foolish and so ashamed."

Earlier in the book I cited the *sense of entitlement* as a pernicious consequence of vitimization. It occurs in the train of downward victimization (denigration and deprivation) and of upward victimization (worship and indulgence). The sense of entitlement includes a series of selective immunities from common tasks and responsibilities.

In a later session, Bonnie told me with little-girl shame that she did indeed scatter her underwear and other belongings on the bedroom floor. Suddenly she snapped her head upward, angrily, and said sharply, "Dammit, when we were dating and were first married Jack always said one of the things he liked best about me was that I was laid-back and not up-tight like his mother. He seemed to like my sloppiness and he made games out of picking up my clothes and hiding them. Now he seems disgusted if he finds any of my things out of place." After a pause Bonnie looked at me with candor and said, "I noticed what I just did. I wasn't exactly blaming Jack but I was getting close, wasn't I?" I nodded agreement while thinking to myself, "Yes, Bonnie, you were getting close to blaming someone else but, by noticing that, you're getting closer to being one of us and closer to being free of a special history."

Bonnie "knew" out loud that she could force herself to pick up her clothes, to get better organized, and to start being on time, but she didn't believe that would get to the root of her problem. I agreed. She asked me what else she could do.

I asked Bonnie if she had told Jack about the bathroom revelation by her friends or about the recollections from childhood. She blanched and blurted with alarm, "I couldn't do that!" I remained quiet while she reheard and re-felt that emerging response. Finally she said, "That's amazing. A picture just came into my head — it was of me looking at Jack looking at me with so much love at his college reunion the year after we were married. He was so proud that I was his wife. I always thought Jack got a lot of his self-esteem from being with me, but I thought that was all right — that it was a sign of love. Maybe it's not all right. But I still can't imagine telling Jack what my girlfriends said. Do you think I should?"

In psychiatrically-correct fashion I hedged my reply, "I don't know about should. But I do believe that telling one's truth is usually healing. (A truer truth in my reply would have been, "Yes, I think you *should* — in the same way that I think you should eat healthy food and get plenty of exercise and plenty of rest." The truth is that telling the truth is necessary for the recovery and maintenance of health.)

Some weeks later when Bonnie, in spite of suffocating anxiety, shared the fateful toilet-stall disclosures with Jack, he burst into tears and hugged her fiercely. "You *are* a helluva woman, Bonnie O!" He said it with level admiration.

After that Bonnie needed little urging to join a psychotherapy group. After a few false-starts at recreating the group in the image of her original family, Bonnie capitalized on her brightness, her history of making lives better, and her support from newly in-love-again Jack. In the group she learned about the benefits of sloppiness and procrastination and tardiness — how these behaviors revived the comforting album of her parents' voices and faces — chiding her indulgently. She slowly crept up on her abiding sense of superiority. One day in group one of the other members confessed to feeling superior. Immediately Bonnie shouted loudly, "I bet I've got a worse case of that than yours." The group erupted into laughter — a moment later Bonnie caught on to her claim of superior superiority. She dissolved with merriment, liberated by absurdity.

Bonnie worked steadily in the group until her departure eighteen months later. By the time she left she had exchanged the rôle of "everyone's darling" for the reality of being a well-loved friend of everyone in the group. She was building true contemporary friendships outside the group simultaneously, substituting those for the private revivals of her early family members. She had further separated psychologically from her parents by uncovering the anger she harbored about being "made special" and by uncovering the sadness of losing her "ordinary" childhood. Somewhere along the way Bonnie told the group that she thought it was easier for her to tell the simple painful truth now because truth-telling relieved the life-long burden of being extraordinary. For the rest of us in the group it was lovely to watch Bonnie replace her hitherto grandly generalized love of humankind with close-in and risky empathy. If wonderful can be safely applied in the human scene it is at such a point of observation — the emergence of human ordinariness from the artifices of the extraordinary *is* full of wonder.

Note: Carl Dennis was born in 1939. He is alive and well, and at age 55 he continues to teach and to write humanizing poetry at the State University of New York in Buffalo.

I finished writing the story of "Bonnie" before I realized that I had transposed Mr. Dennis into the father's generation — his and

Bonnie's. I contacted him by telephone and asked permission to move him backwards in time. His response was a mixture of graciousness and amusement. He said, "That'll be fine so long as you footnote the facts and you guarantee that none of your readers will believe I'm one day older than I actually am."

So Carl Dennis's poem appears in my book about the recovery of the True Self through a convergence of literary license, grace, synchronicity, generosity, and truthful fiction.

Chapter 15

THE PAINFUL DIFFICULTY OF CHANGE

AUDEN REMINDS US THAT WE FREQUENTLY CHOOSE RUIN OVER change. If so, that fact is not an indictment of perversity so much as it is testimony to the pain and difficulty involved in changing one's psychological structure and habit pattern. One reason that psychotherapy is a formidable and time-requiring process is because of the pain involved; the healthy defenses will allow only so much pain in a given period.

To be born a second time must be far more painful than the first. And the pain for the rebirthing person is matched by the pain of the uncomprehending "environmental container" (the latter-day birthing "mother," the maternal aggregate of one's contemporary family and friends and colleagues).

The pains inherent to psychotherapy (recovery of the True Self) are psychological, physiological, physical, spiritual, and social. The difficulty of psychotherapy is reflected in the amount of sheer repetitive work involved in replacing old habits and reflexes with newly chosen ones.

As one does the voluntary work of discarding injurious relics of the past, the subjective sense is initially that one is losing one's entire past. That prospect inevitably spawns dread, anxiety, guilt, and depression. Those responses which are partly psychological and partly physiological lead in turn to eating and sleeping disorders. Those disruptions erode confidence and encourage social withdrawal. Such a sequence can be tolerated only if there is adequate support and adequate reassurance that the chaos is time-limited. One of the reasons that I so strongly advocate group psychotherapy is because of the store of credible reassurance and support available to the newcomer from the veteran members.

Although the early phase of psychotherapy is the most confusing and disorienting, there will be fear and pain as companions to every new insight throughout the course of therapy.

Insight as to origins and visions of remedy always run far ahead of securely installed new structure. That fact of life causes discouragement initially but eventually the patient settles for recurrent frustration, offset by the recognition of new patterns of change and growth.

The cultural wisdoms of school and church and home conspire to caution that growth and development follows a pattern of "two steps forward, one step back." Unfortunately that promised ratio is rarely realized. More often it is "two steps forward and two steps back" or even "one step forward and three steps back." Most refugees from society enter psychotherapy with a linear arithmetic mind-set. To that mentality, the negative ratio of forward-backward is appalling and disillusioning. People can relearn the natural laws of exploration-and-return, of novelty-and-assimilation, and of the gradualism required in revising structure. People can also learn to solicit extra support when they are growing rapidly and when they are on some unfamiliar frontier.

It is poignant to observe how regularly newcomers in group therapy repeat their ancient patterns of adaptation initially, working zealously to be "a good group member" and to be accepted. They have spent a lifetime, for example, taking turns, and being fair. Now they are alien petitioners in a microcosm where many of the trained norms are reversed and all of them are challenged. In the True Self system expression replaces suppression, kindness replaces "niceness," spontaneity replaces regulation, and justice replaces fairness. Those are easy rubrics but replacing requires work, work, work — repetitive, scary, and painful.

Most people come into psychotherapy burdened by the myth of "fairness." The myth is presumably promoted and maintained by adults who refuse to accept the reality of randomness in the universe, and by parents who hope to blunt sibling rivalry by dispensing equity and "fairness." Not only is that spurious ideal of "fairness" unattainable but its pursuit frequently substitutes for attention to justice, redress, and recompense.

At any rate the psychotherapy patient is frequently slowed in his liberation by two applications of the doctrine of "fairness." One, which surely elicits some humane sympathy, is expressed by the person who says with genuine regret, "somehow it doesn't seem right for me to have all this (attention, insight, companionship, opportunity, etc.) when my father didn't . . . brother doesn't . . . wife can't, etc." The alternative is what we call "keeping down with the Joneses." The other application of the "fairness" issue in its "unfair" form comes from recognition by the patient that she is having to do all this painful work in mid-life because of having been mistreated in early life. "It's like being punished for being punished, and that's not fair!"

Initially as one learns the unhealthiness of accustomed speech and behavior and mood there is an awkward self-conscious monitoring. It will be a while before the new patient can move from "catching himself" in the old behaviors to the more appealing and humanizing activity of simply being mindful and of substituting.

A circulating anecdote quotes Eric Berne saying that when he finally finished the manuscript for "Games People Play" he went to bed excited at the prospect of telephoning the news to his friends the next morning. But when he awakened he had the depressing realization that he actually didn't have any friends, only complementary game-players!

Whether that story is true or not, it is certainly true that anyone who undertakes to recover her True Self will find many long-standing "friendships" no longer compatible because they were based on collusive arrangements of co-dependency. Regardless of the inventory, separation from established relationships and social structures is painful.

Finally as one recovers there is a predictable upsurge of creativity, yearnings for adventure, and increased ambition. To venture exposing these newly available energies is painfully scary. We all remember too well the wet blanket response to our childhood creations.

Chapter 16

THE RECOVERY OF THE TRUE SELF
(PSYCHOTHERAPY)

PSYCHOTHERAPY IS THE SPECIFIC TREATMENT PROGRAM FOR recovery of the True Self as director of one's life. That therapeutic program involves two operations which proceed simultaneously; first, the dismantling of the False Self System, and second, the rebuilding of the True Self System. Initially the larger assignment is the dismantling, but as recovery proceeds more and more attention is given to building-in the new True Self reflexes and habit patterns.

Because the process of psychotherapy is so poorly understood and because it is so comprehensive, it will be useful to outline the two-part program and then give detailed commentaries on the line-items.

A.   Dismantling the False Self System
    (1)   Confronting discounts and grandiosities
    (2)   Uncovering the script and the core illusions
    (3)   Analyzing the benefits of dysfunctional patterns
    (4)   Analyzing the dynamics of the family of origin
    (5)   Confronting introjected (incorporated) interactions
    (6)   Reclaiming projections and disavowals

(7) Identifying patterns of abuse (absorption and infliction)
(8) Forgiveness
(9) Grieving
(10) Separating from unhealthy persons and environments

B. Recovering the True Self System
(1) Speaking personal truth
(2) Experimenting with new behaviors
(3) Practicing discipline
(4) Re-learning to ask
(5) Developing healthy support (soothing and comforting)
(6) Going inward (meditation, prayer, solitude)
(7) Substituting
(8) Recovering access to one's affects and emotions
(9) Developing an open-system perspective

Confronting Discounts and Grandiosities

The False Self System was established and it is maintained by traffic in discounting and grandiose exaggerations. Children are unrealistically put down (diminished) or put on a pedestal (elevated). Both behaviors serve unhealthy ends for the parents, the one creating a scapegoat to blame and the other appointing a savior. Both behaviors imprint false identities and they also promote co-dependent rather than reciprocally interdependent relationships.

So the first order of business in my therapeutic program is training in detecting and challenging discounts and exaggerations, whether they come from one's own mouth or someone else's. This training is mechanical and rote initially and it is invariably tainted by the False Self posture of policing and "catching." It is a new behavior occurring before it "feels right." The effort is eventually rewarded by the pleasure one takes in simple truthful and clear communication. As with all new behaviors, there will be some accompanying anxiety and depression, as one violates the old family training.

Uncovering the Script and the Core Illusions

Since all elements of the False Self System are interconnected, the dismantling of any one of the constituent behaviors "loosens up" all the other False Self structures. So when one begins to challenge discounts and exaggerations, not only does one experience anxiety and depression, but one is also assailed by a chorus of "voices" from the past — restraining and inhibiting messages from the family-of-origin are revived and broadcast in the form of internal criticism, skepticism, second-guessing and actual threat. Labeled accusations like "Quitter" or "Traitor" are common. Thus the entire script apparatus (the aggregate of counter-natural messages), which ordinarily operates unconsciously, is exposed to the light of day and to the scrutiny of reason. Some of the core illusions which come to light involve the assumed omniscience of the parents ("I know you will be a success.. a failure . . . a writer . . . a drunkard . . . someone who makes me proud . . . a coward . . . etc.") Other illusions have persuaded the person that disobedience of the parental rules will result in catastrophic outcome — illness, or ruin, or death of the person or the parents or both. And the major illusion common to all the scripts is that acceptance of one's abusive fate will issue in great reward. In point of fact it is only when one begins to reject abuse (discounts and exaggerations, criticism, and manipulations) that one's life gets rewarded.

Analyzing the Benefits of Dysfunctional Patterns

Talk of liberation from the False Self System sounds exciting, but one must count the cost in pain, disorientation, and disillusionment involved in that most profound voluntary separation available to the human animal.

It is an easy matter for me to speak of the clear differences and distinctions between False Self and True Self, but it is not so simple or obvious to the patient. The demarcations between False and True are not subjectively clear, so when the False Self structure begins to collapse, it feels like one's total structure is collapsing.

In my part of the South, the native wisteria vine is a mixed blessing of fragrance and extravagance. Its tentacles proliferate into the earth and they climb the full height of adjacent trees of other species, especially favoring the pine. In the springtime where a well-established wisteria network has all but taken over a pine grove it appears that the pines have been transformed under a heavily perfumed canopy of purple-blue wisteria blossoms. Stopping by such a grove one day to examine close-up the boa-like vines constricting the pine trees, I recognized a natural metaphor for the False Self System. The sweet-smelling wisteria makes a fine show while parasitically merging with the upright but plain-looking pine tree.

Any, effort to separate the tenacious vines from the invaded pine bark offers a sympathetic parallel to the task of dismantling the False Self System. The cleavage planes between vine and bark are not clear and large chunks of pine bark are wrenched away when the vines are stripped off. That liberating removal of the suffocating vines must be very painful for the pine tree.

Understanding the script apparatus allows for conscious choice to reject the false instructions and to resume the natural True Self direction. Resistance to making that choice is always encountered because of the painful difficulty of change. It is at the point of recognizing the resistance that one can profitably make an inventory of the benefits of "staying stuck," i.e. of not changing. That project is enhanced if the person is encouraged to sympathetically honor the resistance rather than criticizing it.

Analyzing the Dynamics of the Family of Origin

Analysis of the patterns of interaction (the "family dynamics") within the family-of-origin allows a person to reconsider the long-standing assumptions of his special victimization.

As one studies the generationally-transmitted patterns of codependency, passivity, and script-formation, it is possible to sympathetically appreciate the childhoods of one's own parents. Blame, a necessary ingredient in the False Self System, becomes increasingly irrelevant when one recognizes first-hand how difficult it is to change, how difficult it is to convert good intentions into amendment of life. Eventually the truism that one's parents "did the best they could" becomes a matter of accepted fact more than a matter of denial or of sentimentality.

Confronting Introjected Interactions

To some extent all the foregoing elements in the dismantling program are informational and educational. The item in the outline identified as "confronting introjected interactions" needs translation. It also needs special emphasis because it is the most exacting task in the recovery process, exacting for the patient and for the therapist.

Remember that the individual's False Self System is established by parental takeover of the child's natural self-actualizing nuclear instructions. The parents (and parental representatives) intrude false identities, false expectations, false limitations, false dependencies, and false information about life into the developing child. The parents employ threat, force, seduction, manipulation, extortion, promise, and bribery to enlist the child in the co-dependent False Self System. And the child inevitably internalizes (incorporates) not only the false messages and instructions but the parents' intruding behaviors as well. And to further complicate the process of internalization, the child also takes in the specific historical *interaction* between himself and the parent. Subsequently the subject person can and will "play the part" of the child *or* of the parent in that two-person loop when a contemporary stimulus revives the original interactional pattern. So an incidental authority-figure today who has no real influence on the person might stimulate the revival of the intimidated "child," or an incidental obstreperous child might mobilize one's restraining "parent." When you observe yourself reflexly behaving as a historical replica, that phenomenon is the daylight version of the nighttime dreamer observing himself within the dream.

"Dynamic psychotherapy" is a generic term specifying those therapies which see these processes of internalization-incorporation-introjection as central in human psycho-pathology, and the address of those processes as pivotal in psychotherapy. Psychoanalysis has relied on the "transference" phenomenon to expose that pathology and to provide the opportunity for remedy. The "transference" is understood as that process in which the patient "projects" on to the therapist those "introjected" internalizations from the original parental structure. In the fully-developed "transference neurosis" the patient replays both sides, the "child" and the "parent," and the historical interaction with its closed-system repetitiveness. Hopefully the analyst/therapist will avoid "playing" the roles predicted by the patient's script and the therapist's dispassionate, disinterested, empathic, and reality-based responses will intervene and modify the "stuck-in-a-groove" repetitions.

This model from psychoanalysis of the particularity of the injury from internalization and of the remedial program is the historical model from which all "dynamic" psychotherapies derive. During the almost-one hundred years since its inception psychoanalytic theory has undergone evolving revisions, and the various dynamic therapies have regularly sought less laborious and less time-consuming methods to liberate patients from the repetition-compulsion. The development of the "transference neurosis" and the subsequent "working through" to increasingly realistic perceptions has required many years of high-frequency high-intensity work.

I believe that psychoanalytic treatment has suffered from its own well-intended patterns of frequency and intensity which promoted an almost cultic isolation. Psychoanalysis "discovered" the repetition-compulsion and other unconscious processes which so dominate and deviate the natural behavior of the human animal. Efforts to share that discovery were met more by skepticism and resistance than by acceptance. Not surprisingly then the devotees of psychoanalysis, both the practitioners and the patients, were driven into a specialized community, increasingly removed from "the ordinary."

And with dire consequences, I believe, psychoanalysis has typically paid insufficient attention to the environment and its continuing influence. The corollary has been an excessive attention, almost perfectionistic, to the internal intrapsychic structure. Another un-natural imbalance.

In theory and in practice classical psychoanalysis promoted and encouraged *compartmentalization* of the treatment program, separating it "for the time being" from the diluting effects of one's on-going life. I am sympathetic to the intent of that requirement, but I believe it violates the natural processes of wound-healing. And for that reason I propose a treatment program that as nearly as possible coincides with ordinary on-going life and as faithfully as possible follows the pattern of biological wound-healing.

Three therapeutic programs which have tried to "speed things up" by essentially by-passing the transference neurosis are those devised by Gestalt Therapy, Psychodrama, and Transactional Analysis. Their technical efforts are frequently more dramatic than sustainable, and they generally rely more on the creativity of the therapist than on the timely re-emergence of the patient's True Self. All three of those programs re-enact some "early scene" or early patterning from the patient's childhood with the idea of providing a decisive contemporary intervention in the closed-system repetition-compulsion. In common the three invoke some combination of cognitive grasp and emotional responsiveness to the historical replay.

Transactional Analysis which is a highly intellectualized

cognitive program proposes a radical "re-decision" as the decisive intervention. A "re-decision" which rejects the original decision to join the co-dependent collusion is indeed necessary for liberation and healing, but it can't be done in a once-and-for-all manner. All of these approaches are useful so long as they are understood as representational and incrementally healing rather than as curative.

In addressing the crucial stuckness of the repetition-compulsion, I draw on my training in medical biology, psychoanalytic theory, Gestalt therapy, psychodrama, transactional analysis, general systems theory, and existential therapy, along with exposures to the healing philosophies of the East and of the indigenous peoples. All of that contributes to a program which is deliberately more "ordinary" than the esoteric form of psychoanalysis and which is studiedly more patient than the dramatic "early-scene" programs.

I believe that psychodynamic group psychotherapy is the most useful format in which people can be liberated from the ancient internalized co-dependencies. Along with psycho-analysis and the three "early-scene" derivatives, I too believe that one's introjections must be projected into the therapeutic arena in order to be revised and then recovered in natural healthy form. However I believe that recovery can only follow the natural biological laws of wound-healing. And that all effective psychosocial activity involved in psychotherapy must parallel the laws of tissue-healing. My understanding is that one must project one's toxic introjections incrementally and repeatedly. One regains health slowly by rebuilding one's own healthy container, progressively defining one's own boundaries, capacities, and limitations. Concretely that means rejecting the falsehood of toxic discounts and grandiosities which falsely define those realities.

To illustrate revision of the repetition-compulsion (or the script) in group psychotherapy we can draw on the earlier accounts of Sandra (Chapter 5) and of Al (Chapter 11).

Recall Sandra's explosive confrontation of Millie, the moral watchdog of their therapy group. Millie's relationship with Sandra initially flourished under Millie's affectionate and maternal wing. However when the monitoring underside of Millie's mothering triggered memories of Sandra's mother intrusively shaming her, the introjected energy of that long-ago humiliation was forcefully projected onto the latter-day surrogate. With matured perspective and reliable support from the group Sandra was able to up-date and substantially modify the closed-system introjection.

From the story of Al you will remember that he was eventually able to recognize his projections onto the new department chairman, but only after his suppression of those light-seeking energies caused him phobic symptoms. I also indicated that Al used the group setting to confront me as authority-surrogate. Group psychotherapy offers many more provocations for the arousal of petrified introjections than does individual therapy. Sandra's principal opportunity for revision came in relation to a peer member, Al's in interaction with the group leader. If one stays in psychoanalysis long enough he will project onto the analyst father energies, mother energies, brother and sister energies, and as well the overall ancient interactional patterns. An advantage to group psychotherapy is the ready availability, in-the-flesh, of all those necessary recipients of projections.

Reclaiming Projections and Disavowals

When falsehood about a child, either as diminution or as elevation, is intruded into that child by the parental structure, "something" which is alien and un-natural is incorporated by the child and eventually seems "natural" or inherent. "They say that's the way I am; that must be the way I am."

Alien incorporation distorts identity, energy expenditure, and personal creativity. It replaces a portion of the child's unique repertoire of gifts, talents, fantasises, dreams, and aspirations. Replacement means that not only is some alien attribute or instruction *added*, but in parallel some natural attributes and personal nuclear instructions must be *disavowed* by denial of their existence or by projecting them into the environment.

Children are taught not only to disavow their "negative" qualities but their positive ones as well. So anger and envy and competitiveness and natural appetites are suppressed at the expense of assertiveness and ambition and healthy patterns of diet and of sexuality. If a child is labeled as "mean" or "selfish" he will eventually incorporate the label. If he believes that he is inherently "mean" then he must suppress and deny all his natural inclinations toward kind and helpful affiliation. If he is labeled "stupid," he must hide his intelligence.

In restoring the nuclear instructions of one's True Self through dismantling and recovery it will be necessary for the person to repetitively practice recalling the projected realities and avowing the disavowed.

In restorative psychotherapy when a formerly "mean" person is daring some altruistic concern or kindness, it is useful to have that new behavior publicly (in a therapy group, for instance) recognized and then verbally acknowledged by the recovering person. "Yes, I am a kind person."

The healing work of psychotherapy does not involve some magical alchemy by which trash is transformed into treasure. Rather it requires the rigorous and regular work of restoring that which was always there. Most patients enter psychotherapy persuaded that they must change completely who and what they are. A more useful perspective is that they need to become more and more who they essentially are.

Identifying Patterns of Abuse (acceptance and infliction)

Interpersonal relationships in the False Self Systems are characterized by the infliction and acceptance of some degree of abuse. The same is true of the individual's relationship in the vocational workplace, in civic and religious organizations, and in respect to the government and culture at large.

The victimizations, inflicted and accepted, are frequently denied, rationalized, or unrecognized. Throughout society various "wisdoms" are bandied about to deny the impact of abuse and so support the unbalanced status quo:

"This hurts me worse than it hurts you."

"This is for your own good."

"People like that are not worth your anger."

"Don't sink to their level; don't let it get to you."

"That kind of stuff doesn't bother me."

'That's your problem."

"An eye for an eye and a tooth for a tooth."

"A soft answer turneth away wrath."

"Someday they'll understand."

"He/she/they will get their comeuppance at the Judgment Day."

"If you truly love you can love any person into change."

The False Self System, like all closed system operations, depends on the dialectic of action and reaction with inevitable consequences of struggle for control. The True Self System depends on dialogue rather than dialectic, on consultation and negotiation in which everyone grows and gains.

In the dismantling and recovery processes it is necessary for the person to identify and confront all patterns and instances of exploitation and abuse, whether they arise from the environment or from oneself. Protesting environmental abuse will not eliminate all abuse, but protest will undo the acculturated falsehood that abuse is tolerable. And remembering the principle that no energy can be gotten rid of but rather can be transformed, it is necessary to substitute and replace the abusive energy with nurturing energy.

The recovering human animal is almost ready to discard the False Self System when he recognizes that he is still clinging to the familiar patterns of abuse as well as being held on to by the abusers. And the human animal is indeed ready to replace the False Self System with True Self direction when she can say, "I am now willing to take the scary step of giving and receiving only abuse-free love."

Forgiveness

It is said that forgiveness is "love's divinest portion." Apart from the moral and poetic ring of that claim, I am persuaded that forgiveness is an ultimate achievement of psycho-spiritual maturity and of *self*-love.

To not forgive is to not let go of abuse. Abuse unforgiven is perpetuated in one's consciousness and it regularly triggers fantasies of restitution and revenge. To not forgive is to remain frozen in time — impaled on the moment of the wounding, yesterday or yesteryear.

Alice Miller, a Swiss psychoanalyst, has devoted her recent career to publicizing and exposing the common abusiveness of family life toward children. Her book "For Your Own Good" [13] is sub-titled "Hidden Cruelty in Child-Rearing and the Roots of Violence." In this volume she carefully describes and documents the common patterns of generationally-repeated abuse and violence. And she urges the daunting remedy of forgiveness as the only effective intervention in that repetitive pattern.

In a compelling summary Miller writes:

> "Religion says we must forgive the injustice we suffered; only then will we be free to love and be purged of hatred. This is correct as far as it goes, but how do we find the path of true forgiveness? Can we speak of forgiveness if we hardly know what was actually done to us and why? And that is the situation we found ourselves in as children."
>
> "We could not grasp why we were being humiliated, brushed aside, intimidated, laughed at, treated like an object, played with like a doll or brutally beaten (or both). What is more, we were not even allowed to be aware that all this was happening to us, for any mistreatment was

held up to us as being necessary for our own good." (Note: In her litany of injuries, Miller does not here include the life-threatening wound of elevation/grandiosity which is especially dangerous because it has the seductive trappings of special nurturance.)

"Even the most clever child cannot see through such a lie if it comes from the mouths of beloved parents who, after all, show him other, loving sides as well. He has to believe that the way he is being treated is truly right and good for him, and he will not hold it against his parents. But then as an adult he will act the same way toward his own children, in an attempt to prove to himself that his parents behaved correctly toward him."

"Isn't this what most religions mean by "forgiveness": to chastise children "lovingly" in the tradition of the fathers and to raise them to respect their parents? But forgiveness which is based on denial of the truth and which uses a defenseless child as an outlet for resentment is not true forgiveness. That is why hatred is not vanquished by religions in this manner but, on the contrary, is unwittingly exacerbated."

"The child's intense anger at the parents, being strictly forbidden, is simply deflected onto other people and onto himself, but not done away with. Instead, because it is permissible to discharge this anger onto one's own children, it spreads over the entire world like plague. For this reason we should not be surprised that there are religious wars, although such a phenomenon should actually be a contradiction in terms."

Genuine forgiveness does not deny anger but faces it head-on. If I can feel outrage at the injustice I have suffered, can recognize my persecution as such, and can acknowledge and hate my persecutor for what he or she has done, only then will the way of forgiveness be open to me."

"Only if the history of abuse in earliest childhood be uncovered will the repressed anger, rage, and hatred cease to be perpetuated. Instead they will be *transformed* into sorrow and pain at the fact that things had to be that way. As a result of this pain, they will give way to genuine understanding, the understanding of an adult who has now gained insight into his or her own parent's childhoods and finally, liberated from his own hatred, can experience genuine, mature sympathy."

"Such forgiveness cannot be coerced by rules and commandments; it is experienced as a form of grace and appears spontaneously when a repressed (because forbidden) hatred no longer poisons the soul. The sun does not need to be told to shine. When the clouds part, it simply shines. But it would be a mistake to say that the clouds are not in the way if they are indeed there."

"To be free to express resentment dating back to early childhood does not mean that one now becomes a resentful person but rather the exact opposite."

"For these reasons I believe that the free expression of resentment against one's parents represents a great opportunity. It provides access to one's true self, reactivates numbed feelings, opens the way for mourning and — with luck — reconciliation. In any case, it is an essential part of the process of psychic healing."

Miller's explication of the process of forgiveness reflects the hard and painful work involved in that healing. It is obviously a much more profound event than that which is commonly conveyed in the easily-sought easily-offered almost perfunctory exchange of "forgiveness." The experience of genuine forgiveness always involves anxiety, pain, sadness, and anger for both the forgiver and the forgiven.

Grieving

Growthful life includes an unending succession of losses and separations, starting with birth and ending with death. There are losses of the successive stages of infancy and childhood, loss of security, loss of innocence and the carefree state, loss of being preferred, loss of wishes and hopes, loss of opportunity, loss of illusion, and loss of status. One loses pets and toys and friends and parents. Not only the world of childhood, but one's youth and vigor and health are progressively lost or diminished.

The False Self System teaches two un-natural and unhealthy responses to loss. The one discounts the impact of the loss and the other exaggerates it. One promotes an anesthetized "stiff upper lip," and the other exploits the loss as a dramatic victimization which confers entitlement and solicits pity.

I believe that every loss inflicts a two-fold injury to the Person. The Ego, which is the object-relating organ, loses something to which it was attached and in which it was invested. The Self, which is not invested in the environment, nevertheless suffers a narcissistic loss in the experience of vulnerability.

Healing the wound of loss requires that both the Ego's loss and the Self's loss be recognized and honored. Here I make a distinction between mourning and grieving. Mourning is the remedial response to the Ego's loss and it is best experienced in the company of others; attention is focused mainly on the lost object (pet, parent, job, health). Grieving is the remedial response to the Self's loss and it is best experienced in solitude; attention is focused mainly on the Self who has experienced the loss. In solitude one learns to feel sorrow for one's Self. That empathic sorrow is restorative and it is in sharp contrast to the style of solicited pity in the False Self System which teaches people to unhealthily "feel sorry for themselves," in a maudlin posture.

In the dismantling of the False Self System mourning and grieving and forgiveness are all interconnected elements in the process of "letting go," of finishing unfinished business.

A prerequisite in exchanging the True Self System for the False is that *sadness* be restored to a place of honor in one's emotional experience. Only if one recovers sensitivity to one's own pain and sadness can that person be open to the full richness and joy of life.

Hanna Segal, [14] who was a notable member of the British psychoanalytic "school of object-relations," reported a remarkable dream shared by a woman patient. The dream and

Segal's interpretations capture the crucial issues of loss, mourning, grieving, and forgiveness. The dreamer was much improved, Segal writes, after several years of analysis and she was considering termination.

"She dreamt that she was driving her car to work. There was some anxiety at this point because the electric current was cut off, but she realized that she had a torch battery (flashlight) of her own and that the battery was in working order. When she arrived at work she waited for a doctor to turn up to help her; but when he turned up he had a broken arm in a sling and was useless. She slowly realized that the work she was supposed to carry out was the opening of an enormous mass grave. She started digging alone by the light of her little torch. Gradually, as she dug, she realized that not all the people buried in this grave were dead. Moreover, to her great encouragement, those who were still alive immediately began to dig with her. At the end of the dream, she had a very strong feeling that two things had been achieved; one was that anyone who was still alive had been rescued from this mass grave, and had become her helper; and secondly, that those people who were dead could now be taken out of the anonymous grave and could now be buried properly with their names on the grave.

Briefly, this dream represented to her the gradual solving of her depressive anxieties. Going to work with her little torch meant facing by herself the full extent of her depressive situation, facing her vicious attacks on her mother and all the mother representatives, which led to the mass grave inside her, the anonymous depression, when she did not know what she was mourning for.

The work of mourning in this dream consisted of rescuing and restoring what could be rescued and restored. The objects which she had restored immediately turned into helpers; that is the objects first destroyed by her and then restored became assimilated by her and strengthened her own ego.

But not everything that had been destroyed could be restored. She also had to face those situations in which the object was really dead, like many of her relatives, and situations in which she felt she had done harm which could not be undone. And here the important point is that each of those situations and persons had to be properly named and buried, that is, they had to be recognized and mourned without denial, not lost in a mass grave. When properly buried they could eventually be given up and did not have to be kept magically alive, so that the patient's libido (i.e. attachment energy) might be free of her fixation on them."

Speaking Personal Truth

In recovering and maintaining the True Self System it is necessary for one to speak the Truth.

The scholars distinguish between "propositional" truth (scientific reality) and "personal" truth (subjective reality). In recovering self-direction one must speak both kinds of truth. In the False Self System propositional truth is violated by diminutions (discounts) and enlargements (grandiosities), and personal truth is distorted by the pretenses and illusions of co-dependency.

In the course of socialization and the implantation of the False Self System our Ego-boundaries have been damaged. When we discount ("That didn't hurt me.") we form a desensitized callous over part of our boundary. When we exaggerate ("My life is ruined.") we open wide an aperture for hysterical exchange (the prelude to "Panic Disorder").

When we speak the simple factual truth, especially about our independent experience of the moment, we re-draw our boundaries more nearly in their original structure of firm flexibility.

Remembering the basic relationship between the boundary-ing (containing) Ego and the contained Self, you will appreciate the happy fact that every time you speak a "boundary truth" (e.g. "that hurts," or "I want one of those," or "that doesn't fit.") you also define your Self. If I lost contact with my True Self by dependent adaptation, by pretense and denial and disguise, I shall recover True self-direction by declaring what I want, what I don't want, what I feel emotionally, what I yearn for, and what my intuition and senses tell me (e.g. "I see that the emperor has no clothes today.")

As I indicated earlier the processes of dismantling and recovery occur simultaneously as well as in sequence. The line-item breakdown I provided is not intended to represent some fixed sequence of restoration. However it is true that in recovering the True Self direction there is a preponderance of dismantling early on. Specifically, given the starting-point of recognizing one's immersion in the False Self System it is necessary initially to say "no" more often than one says "Yes." That is, the first order of restorative business is to interrupt the inflictions and abuses, so one must say frequently, "I don't want...," before he can confidently say, "What I want is ..."

Experimenting with new Behavior

All human behavior both momentary and sustained, involves neurological, vascular, chemical, gaseous, hormonal, musculoskeletal, cognitive-perceptual, and psychological activity simultaneously. And all these component functions are interconnected; they individually influence all the others and they are synchronized with each other. Their interactional sequences establish reflexes and habit patterns. The maturing human animal progressively builds in the conditioned sequences which are "grooved" in the person's bio-psycho-physiology.

Changing behavior patterns requires "re-grooving" of sequences which are consummated in a desired outcome.

Insight provides a view (a retrospective sighting) of the origins of dysfunctional behavior, and it provides a vision of alternatives or options which "turn-out better." But insight alone does not change the patterned reflexes and familiar habitual responses. Change requires the repetitive work of building in new bio-psychophysiological reflexes. It involves trying-out, experimenting with, and practicing the envisioned new behavior before it is well-grooved; all such efforts are initially awkward, frustrating, and discouraging. They will be sustained only with encouragement, praise for incremental growth, and patience.

Persons who have been taught in their families-of-origin to deflect or reject compliments will initially have great difficulty learning to solicit and accept recognition and congratulations for healthy changes.

Changing to healthier patterns of thinking, feeling, contacting, and communicating is considerably more difficult and awkward then learning to ride a bicycle or to ski, but the eventual gracefulness of the harvested changes is far more rewarding than the acquisition of new motor skills. When we become coordinated and graceful in any new activity we say, "I can now do this by second nature." The resumption of healthy functioning (or recovery of the True Self System) is actually a return to "first nature." But that return requires work, work, work — practice, practice, practice.

Practicing Discipline

Discipline is defined as "Training that is expected to produce a specified character or pattern of behavior, especially that which is expected to produce moral or mental improvement." [15] Alternative definitions include various aspects of programs which either teach or punish.

One reason that the socialized human animal resists accepting discipline and practicing it for oneself is because of the frequent experience of discipline as punishment or as arbitrary restriction by various parental structures.

I urge the practice of discipline in the deliberate recovery of the True Self System for a purpose other than instruction or "improvement" or punishment. I promote discipline because it is a prerequisite for reconstructing a healthy Container.

Recall from the earlier descriptions of the containing Ego

(Chapter 7) that some cardinal characteristics of a healthy container are reliability, consistency, flexibility, softness, and toughness. When a fortunate child is reared in a healthily containing family she is taught by patient repetition and she is reassured by regularity. If a child cannot rely on the containing parental environment for regularity then the child will develop a pattern of impatiently acting-out emerging tension or of becoming discouraged into lassitude. The healthy container (one's parental environment in infancy; one's Ego later) is neither tense-tight nor slack-loose but tonic. As a descriptive term in physiology "tonic" means "of good tone"; it is the condition of the resting muscle which is neither stiff nor flaccid but "on the ready."

The discipline required for physical conditioning is a suitable model for the more comprehensive disciplines of rebuilding a tonic Ego container. When one undertakes discipline as a voluntary opportunity rather than as an externally imposed requirement or a hateful duty, then one has the liberating sense of re-creating one's own life.

Self-engaged discipline promotes a self-reliance which leads to a more expectant relationship with the environment. This is in contradistinction to a form of exaggerated self-reliant self-sufficiency which is counterdependent and socially isolating.

The self-disciplined person does not have to worry about his own reliability. He can awake each day assured that he will not explode impulsively nor falter in the repetitive requirements of adult living. His tonic container propels him out of restful sleep into a zestful engagement with the environments of people and Nature. He will flexibly regulate his own rhythms of work and play and rest and solitude and interpersonal contact. With a gentle voice and level eyes, he will frequently say to himself and others, "No!"

Re-Learning to Ask

Having been disappointed, rebuffed, diverted, deferred, and chided for clear expression of wants/wishes/desires, most children grow into adult life having "learned" to not ask directly for what they want.

"It's not polite to ask; wait your turn."

"I'll get it for you later."

"Aren't you ever satisfied?"

"You put people on the spot when you ask directly."

"If you have to ask for it, it loses value. If people really care they'll give it to you without you having to ask."

Child-rearing which teaches people to not ask promotes either an exaggerated self-sufficient independence or a pitiful helpless style which manipulates and extorts.

In recovering True Self initiative people must learn again to dare wants and to request and petition the environment.

For many adults who have finally learned to ward off mistreatment and abuse there is an inclination to settle for that improved state of affairs. Not wanting to "rock the boat" or "push their luck," many survivors decide to "stop while they are (slightly) ahead."

After decades of deprivation, disappointment, and incommensurate reward many people conclude that if "I'm going to get it, I'll have to get it myself." That perspective often leads to patterns of overwork or to schemes of embezzlement and thievery.

The common reality is that people enjoy giving and they are elevated by being asked for something which they can deliver. Given the prevailing rubrics about the superior virtue of giving, it is not surprising that "well-socialized" persons would be loathe to ask to receive. But it is a pleasure watching recovering human animals relearning to satisfy their animal wishes directly in an honoring environment. Recovery is sometimes hastened when people can understand that unbalanced giving is a hurtfully controlling behavior.

Developing Healthy Support

In the prevailing and historically familiar False Self System persons adapt to and settle for interpersonal support which is frequently of poor quality. The ancient formulas of caretaking-mixed-with-abuse come to be the expected norms.

With the same kind of wisdom which allows fragile vegetation to eke out an existence in harsh environments, the human animal learns to survive on suboptimal nutrients. Eric Berne, who enjoyed playing with imaginary numbers, said "It takes one hundred strokes (interpersonal contacts) a day to keep the spinal cord from shriveling up. Positive strokes are preferable but negative ones will do." In a low-risk trade-off many people learn to get most of their human exchanges through rancor, belligerence, complaining, gossiping, intimidation, or whining. Not only do those behaviors "work" to provide stimulation but they also become the exchange commodities of co-dependent relationships with varying degrees of sado-masochistic energy exchanges.

There is no round of rejoicing in the interpersonal environment when a recovering person declares that she will no longer accept abuse as part of an interdependent relationship.

When someone says, in effect, "From this time forward I want encouragement instead of criticism, empathy rather than pity, challenge rather than indulgence, respect rather than discount, confrontation rather than condescension, dialogue instead of dogma, fighting fair instead of feigning forgiveness, tenderness instead of testiness, truth instead of falsehood," most "friends" in the existing circle of "support" will fall away.

Most people are unwilling to forgo the hurtful pleasures of negative communication. We have all been warned about "fair-weather friends." When we return to the True Self orientation we discover an even more hazardous group, "foul-weather friends."

It is daunting to separate from longtime companions who traffic in a mixture of nurture-and-abuse. It is daunting to give up the unhealthy "support" network before we have built a healthy network of our choosing. But choose we must.

In rebuilding a healthful adult supportive network which is truthful and reliable and trustworthy we can follow a model of the ideal child-parent relationship. Now as then we need a healthy container. "They" told us we should be more trusting; finally we discover that what we mainly need is a more trustworthy environment.

While lecturing on this recovery-task recently I noticed a distinction between related forms of support which I believe is useful. Children know about the distinction but most of us adults have forgotten. The two forms of support are reassurance and comfort.

When a child (or adult) is fearful about something in the future (five minutes from now, or Judgement Day, or the possibility of a hurricane) he needs reassurance from accurate statistical information and instructions about safety and recovery. If a child (or adult) has been injured by some event in the past (just now or several years ago) and is still in pain, she needs comfort, preferably in the form of physical holding.

In later life the child whose fears have been soothed by reassurance can supply her own soothing alone as she applies the lessons she learned about reality-testing. One can soothe oneself in this manner but the extent to which one can comfort one's already wounded self is limited; the human animal needs another human animal to supply comfort.

Empathic and sensitive support-people will inquire as to what is needed rather than presuming. They will be available for soothing (reassuring) or comforting (holding).

The particular relationships which we call "interpersonal" comprise only one portion of a person's environment. The "people network" is perhaps the most critical component of the environment which inclines us toward health or unhealth, but other components are vitally important as well.

Nature is restorative. Those human animals, who for a variety of good and bad reasons, live in cities require extra effort to have sustaining on-going relationships with Nature; it behooves them to make that effort.

Recall the earlier (Chapter 8) quotation from Winston Churchill, "We shape our buildings, and afterwards they shape us." That dialectic consequence is true also for the literature, and art, and music, and dance, and film, and machinery which we create. We shape them and afterwards they will surely shape us. If we are wise we will be as discriminating about these highly influential environments as we are becoming about the breathable atmospheric environment.

We need to view crime and violence and war and natural disaster and divorce and industrial devastation of Nature with mobilizing alarm rather than with passive fascination. The ubiquitous television and sensational journalism create an endemic sensory overload which spawns anesthesia, passivity, and a sense of impotent hopelessness.

If we are to participate in the culture, if we are to extend ourselves helpfully into the world of people, we must "keep up with the news." But we must also maintain an autonomous selectivity in what we look at and listen to and read.

In its unending bounty and variety and predictability and surprise and sensory balm, Nature is restorative. So are "good" people. All of the socialized human animals are "good-hyphen-evil" people, but there is a vast army of human beings out there who are mainly good, who mainly express healing energy. I get healthier if look at and listen to and think along with healthy models whom I deliberately select to occupy my immediate sensory environment. For me some models who have inspired are Lou Gehrig, and Mohandas Ghandi, and Dag Hammarskjöld, and Martin Luther King, and Sister Theresa, and Roberta Blackgoat, and Joan Baez; inspiration speaks mainly to the Self or soul. Other models who have been sustaining, that is, supportive of my sensate Ego, are minstrel-philosophers like Mary Chapin-Carpenter and Clint Black, comedians like Bill Cosby and Garrison Keillor whose humor originates in the belly and is kind; athletes and scientists who are disciplined and devoted to excellence like Jackie Joyner-Kersee and Stephen Hawking; and writers like W. H. Auden and William Styron and Peter Matthiessen and Maxine Kumin and Carl Dennis and Ethan Canin who broaden our humanity by sharing their own.

There are many "bad" people out there also. They are False Self persons with unmodified narcissism. There are those who traffic in sadistic humor, politicians who engage in demagoguery and falsehood, entertainers who prostitute their intellect and sexuality for their gain and our loss, journalists who highlight the deviant and degenerate in society, TV interviewers

who violate emotional boundaries, and shameless religious
charlatans. Those people and their subject matter are elements
of reality but for one's own humanization they are not "required
reading."

It is a truism that "what we eat we become." That
observation can be extended to other intake as well: "what we
stare at, listen closely to, inhale, and consort with sensually, we
become."

One of the most precious, powerful, and poorly publicized
freedoms is the freedom of focus. The last of the autonomous
freedoms is that freedom of focus, which is exercised by the eye
muscles, the neck muscles, and the "mind's eye" of imagination.
"They" can lead me to the desecration but they can't force me
to stare at it. If I choose I can preferentially look at beauty and
goodness and growth. If I am to remain healthy I must make
that choice.

Going Inward

The Self is at the center of the Person. The Self is the soul
or the nucleus which provides our autonomous instructions, our
"homing" directions. (Mary Chapin-Carpenter sings in the
ballad "Why Walk When You Can Fly" the recognition that "in
this world you've a soul for a compass, and a heart for a pair
of wings." [16] If we are to recover the Self, to be with the Self,
to become once again Self-directed, we must deliberately turn
away from the outer worlds of our own Ego and of the
Environment and turn inward in solitude.

The Person can visit the Self only through the cooperation
and effort of the Ego. In a remarkable way the Ego makes the
arrangements for the Self to be alone, knowing full-well that the

Ego will of necessity then be sent away! Isn't that indeed what a healthy Parent does repeatedly on behalf of the Child, and what any unconditional lover must do for the beloved? Remember that the Person's container (Ego) is an internalized replica of the original nurturant container.

It is the Ego which announces to the significant other people, "My Self wants to be alone for a while." The Ego finds a place and a time which is suitable and the Ego is satisfied that the location is safe and that she/he (Ego) will not be distracted from protective vigilance while the Person is inside with her/his Self. The Ego suspends thinking (planning, fantasizing, checking lists, or reminiscing) and becomes devoted to vigilant sensitivity.

Meditation as a practice is the disciplined pattern of regularly going-inward. There are also other occasions when the wise person will arrange to be with the Self. Those are the occasions when one knows that for whatever reason there has been a build-up, an accumulation, of unexpressed feeling. People recognize such an occasion when they say, "I want to scream!" Hopefully that person's Ego will take that declaration seriously and will make the logistical arrangements for the person to scream whatever wants to come out; it might be rage or grief or joy.

The Ego encourages the Person to meditate and to pray and to "go into the woods" to scream, or bellow, or sob, or exult. By agreement the Ego waits outside (outside the inner sanctum or outside "the screaming place").

Both the regular practice of being-with-Self and the ad hoc withdrawal for intentional Self-explosion need to be experienced in solitude. Solitude is not isolation or defensive aloneness; it is the protected separation of Self and Ego and Environment.

To recovering people I recommend the regular discipline of going-inside, at least once a day, and as well practicing "undress" rehearsals for the ad hoc explosions.

In order to go inside and be with the Self there must be a cooperative and gradual separation of Ego and Self. What this means in ordinary language is that the Person must deliberately suspend Ego activities, primarily movement and verbal-intellectual activity. But we cannot stop thinking by thinking about that project. We can only substitute in our focus and we do that in retrograde fashion, moving from the brain to the body and finally to the spirit (soul, Self). We can stop noticing our thoughts and their verbal-visual associations if we focus on the interior of our bodies and especially on our rhythmical breathing function. But breathing is still an intentional Ego-guided activity, so we focus next on Breath which is a gift shared by all animals. We merge with the universe when we focus on universal Breath. And Breath is Spirit and Soul and Self. In all the religions it is Divine Breath which creates life and revives it. The great world religions also teach in common that both the "Kingdom of God" and "eternal life" are inside each person. This is the realization and the gift when one dares to go inside. There is only peace and contentment there; no happiness nor sadness nor desire nor fear exist, because they cannot exist apart from the Ego.

Even a momentary experience of the Self revives and refreshes the whole Person. One can infer from that effortless refreshment just how much energy we use up in our socially-required assignments of keeping Ego and Self (Body and Soul) together. In the Self there is neither time nor space, those prime markers of the Ego and of the workaday world.

The intentional pathway to the Self has been explored and elaborated by devotees of Eastern religions and by the world's indigenous peoples. The drumming and chanting and humming and the repetitive recitations of the universal sound "AUM" all replicate biological beats and rhythms and they serve to usher one from body to soul.

Focusing on an open fire or gazing at an occulting light has a trance-inducing effect on the human animal. These activities remind one of the existence of the Soul, but they do not readily lead to it because their stimulation is obviously external and sensory (Ego-bound). The same can be said about the votary use of incense and about sweat-lodge experiences, about flowing water and oceans and mountain vistas, and about yoga and Tai Chi; healthful though they are those experiences incline one toward gratitude and worship. Gratitude and worship are both healing, but they are relational and communal (even if the community is only I-and-Thou) and they cannot substitute for the solitary Self-finding experience.

Substituting

In previous sections I have stressed many times (but not yet too many) that nothing (no particle of energy) can be removed or gotten rid of. A particular energy (thought, attitude, mood, gesture, emotional expression, motor pattern, habit, etc .... etc.) can be replaced by another form of one's choosing. One cannot eliminate an undesirable energy but one can replace it by substitution. There are numerous fables, tales, and wisdom lessons which teach the futility of driving out or exorcising "demons" with no replacement. After a brief respite, earned by will-power, the demons return with reinforcements!

Indeed the recovery of the True Self direction requires substituting the original natural system for the acquired False

Self System. That requirement applies to the full system and to its various components. So a society cannot rid itself of warmaking; it could successfully substitute assertive peace-making. A person cannot get rid of depression but he can substitute the natural energy of grieving-sadness. No one can simply stop a "bad" habit; it can only be replaced by a "good habit."

Substitution requires work, lots of work, retraining one's grooved neuromuscular equipment to react differently to problematic stimuli in the environment.

Recovering Access to One's Affects and Emotions

Socialization and the establishment of the False Self System are achieved by the individual's acceptance of a parentally required program of denial, displacement, and desensitizing anesthesia by which one can block awareness of environmental impact.

Persons in psychotherapy, especially in group psychotherapy, learn to progressively reduce the lag time between the injurious stimulus and their affective registry of the injury. In the group's encouraging supportive environment a person might report with well-deserved and hard-earned satisfaction, "I recognized that I was angry at her just a few hours after she said that. It used to be a matter of weeks before I could recognize the blow for what it was."

People in recovery also re-learn the simultaneity of multiple affects, even of opposing ones. Our childhood reports of several feelings coming all at once were frequently met with impatience and distrust: "Well, make up your mind — which is it?"

We were supposed to be consistent. Emerson, [17] at least, knew better. It was he who observed, "A foolish consistency is the hobgoblin of little minds, adored by little statesmen and philosophers and divines. With consistency a great soul has nothing to do." I am grateful for that corrective. He could have added that parentally-required consistency is also a powerful inhibitor of the child's natural and spontaneous affective-emotional life.

As indicated in an earlier chapter, sentimentality is an indiscriminate amalgam of multiple affects, each of which has been disallowed in some measure. Sentimentality is like Hanna Segal's patient's mass grave (page 150); in emotional recovery the specific affects have to be exhumed and named and expressed.

In recovery one also relearns that tearfulness and a choked voice authenticate communications rather than contaminating them. In the False Self System, tears and tremor are marks of weakness rather than certificates of truth. In the False Self System we are taught to value smooth dispassionate speech. Recovery of the True Self restores the natural connection between thought and feeling, between cognitive and emotional responses.

Developing an Open-System Perspective

The True Self System is an open-system which does not pretend the final truthfulness of a single truth.

Recall that the characteristics of open-systems include trial-and-error procedure, false start, overshoot, steady state, and equifinality (which translates, "There are several ways to get from here to there.") In closed systems there is a "set point," a "right" answer, "*the*" truth.

Paradoxically but not surprisingly it is those children who are fortunate enough to be reared in a relatively open system, who are best able and most willing to submit to the limitations and restrictions of closed-system operations when, as in scientific pursuit, the closed-system perspective is the appropriate one.

Mischief is done when the closed-system scientific mechanistic perspective is applied in the interpersonal world. And healing is promoted when people are encouraged to understand "error" and "getting off the path" as opportunity more than as deviation. The opportunities are represented as occasions for tolerance, forgiveness, encouragement, expectation of second chance, and as discovery. You can do an experiment which demonstrates the effect of perspective and attitude on your body and your physiology. The experiment is illuminating, pleasurable, and reassuring. If you will first recite out loud the characteristics of closed systems (set point, linear feed-back, right-wrong, and deterioration) you will notice that your muscles become tense and you experience constriction of your breathing and some anxiety. Then shift to a recitation of open-system vocabulary (trial-and-error, false start, overshoot, second-chance, steady-state, and "lots of ways to get there"). You will notice relaxation of your muscles and buoying of your spirit.

In summary, psychotherapy involves dismantling of the acquired False Self structure and restoring the True Self System. Those two processes proceed simultaneously, with considerable overlap, and with increasing shift from dismantling to recovering.

Although I listed the elements of both processes in line-item sequence, I'll say again that there is no "right" order of appearance of these elements. Particular ones emerge at particular times because of unpredictable stimulus and association from the environment.

Part of the good news is that the recovery of *any* natural

behavior in True Self direction confers some recovery-gain in *all* of the healthy behaviors. So, for example, if one speaks one's personal truth there is simultaneously some open system perception, some increased access to emotion, some substitution, some improvement of support-network, some greater readiness to ask, and so on. To make healthier any one of those behavior areas makes healthier the entire structure.

If the holistic perspective is true, as I believe, then "everything is connected to everything" for the human animal. That truism applies to all of the person's biological and psychological and spiritual systems and as well to the concentric environments of society and culture and Nature. If all of reality is interconnected then at every given moment each human animal, throughout its entire organism, is getting somewhat healthier or somewhat unhealthier.

Most "psychotherapy" programs and the cultural philosophies which undergird them are not about *recovery* but about *relief.*

Dominated as it is by the values of big business, empire-building, and technology our society views illness as a symptomatic interference with performance, productivity, and efficiency. It is the logic of the marketplace to focus on the symptom rather than on the signal. The "signal" aspect of illness is a message from the wisdom of the body about disharmony between the person and the environment. Disharmony and the loss of natural rhythm and balance issue from the human animal's violations of the laws of nature. Such violations are encouraged and even required by a society devoted to achievement, production, profit, and accumulation.

The society-at-large and much of the professional community conceive of psychological illness in fragmented, compartmented, and isolated terms. So a person is said diagnostically to "have" a panic disorder or a depressive illness or a phobia, or to "be" an obsessive-compulsive or an hysteric. All of the diagnostic categories are symptomatic of life in the False Self System. The categories of "mental illness" (except for the tiny fraction attributable to organic injury or defect) are all statements of non-conformity, but the self-interested dominant society hears those statements as "admission" of weakness rather than as health-seeking protest.

Like the controlling Parent in the family-of-origin the societal Parent requires conformity. The societal False Self System supplies a flood-tide of chemical agents (alcohol, tranquilizers, antidepressants, energizers, sleeping potions, and the lethal addictive mood-modifiers) which serve to relieve symptoms, enhance conformity, "peacefully" quell the protester.

It is a great tragedy that psychotherapy has been made (by a consortium of legislators and insurance companies and managed care middlemen, and psychopharmaceutical empires) subservient to the needs of the society. In the False Self System illness is understood as inconvenience rather than opportunity, and symptom is understood as a call for repair rather than for recovery.

Recovery requires two life-moving decisions. First, one must essentially declare the bankruptcy of the False Self System! If that sounds desirable, easy, or obvious, then re-consider. The False Self System was delivered to us by cherished parents and teachers and religious faiths and patriot calls. Secondly, one must decide, on self-interested grounds, to undertake the rigorous discipline of rebuilding one's own Ego.

Self-interest is the "interest" of the Ego in the Self. Self-interest includes healthy self-love and self-empathy.

Recovery of True Self-direction recovers the best of the two human worlds, the world of law and the world of love. In the

False Self System those worlds are regularly set against each other and thus both are contaminated by discounts and grandiosities. The law which is not infused by love becomes ruthless (without "ruth," without compassion). And love unsupported by the law becomes vapid indulgence.

In the book and film "Babette's Feast" the mellowed old general toasts recovery by quoting the couplet from Psalm 85:
"Mercy and truth have met together;
Righteousness and peace have kissed each other."

The process of recovery (for an individual or a population) evolves in a predictable sequence which reverses the history of loss of self-direction. First there is recovery of the senses, a recovery from desensitization and anesthesia. Recovery restores sight to the blinded, hearing to the deafened, smell to the sanitized, touch to the untouched, and voice to the silenced.

Recovery of "voice" is figurative and literal. Persons who regain self-direction speak up, speak their truth, have a voice, voice their wants and their protests. In a literal sense as well, the natural functioning of the vocal cords and the rest of the speech apparatus is restored. Rasping speech becomes smooth, mushy speech becomes articulate, loud speaking softens, the inaudible becomes audible, and the monotone becomes melodic. Beautiful speech is a natural gift.

Recovery of senses is followed by recovery of perspective. Realistic self-appraisal replaces grandiose inflation and discounting diminution. One accepts limitations and appropriates one's capacities and talents on a realistic basis.

Recovery of perspective leads to recovery of identity. Self-instructed identity allows one to discern one's commonality with all other human beings and to identify one's unique and particular differences as well — and to be grateful for both.

Psychological healing from psychological wounding is a natural process like tissue wound-healing, and it cannot be arbitrarily foreshortened. The current push for "brief psychotherapy" not only betrays ignorance of the healing process, but it defies common-sense logic as well. Albeit appealing in concept, no one would openly advocate "brief pregnancy," "brief fracture knitting," or "brief adolescence," all processes governed by the person's True Self nucleus.

Like the convalescence of a wounded child, sustained and sustainable psychotherapy is a natural process. It can be arbitrarily discouraged and even disallowed, but like all natural functions which are neglected, opposed, or driven underground it will sprout again and revive.

Chapter 17

THE HUMAN ANIMAL IN AND OUT OF THERAPY

REGARDLESS OF THE PASSING FATE OF PROFESSIONAL PSYCHO-therapy, the human animal will be perpetually in and out of therapy, in and out of wounding and healing. Sickness, injury, wounding, and death are inevitable; the cycles of recovery and healing are indomitable until death.

In an earlier section (Chapter 10) I described the prevailing models of "how life is" within the False Self System. The false models are named Progress, Puritan, and Heroic. There are secondary models adopted by persons who have recognized the inadequacy of the societal modes; they are called Roller-Coaster, Circular, and Discontinuous.

The True Self System model of "how life is" is the natural model and it has the pictorial configuration of a conical helix.

A few years ago at a meeting of group psychotherapists in New York, the Greek psychiatrist George Vassilliou was talking about the nature of life and he told us that a verbal root related to the word "anthropos" (man) was translated, "to spiral upwards." That association stimulated me to think of the human life-course as helical in design, spiraling upward in continuous but ever-enlarging concentric circles. Several additional structures and refinements led to the model which follows; I call it "The Human Helix."

Unlike the False Self System models, all of which are closed, linear, two-dimensional structures, the helix is open, circular, and three dimensional.

All of the primary false models (Progress, Puritan, and Heroic) describe courses or tracks which the subject is to follow. Those tracks are established by someone else; they "belong" to someone else.

In contrast the helical path is one's own markings and track; from birth to death it is entirely the subject's "possession," like a private highway.

Many clinicians talk of "regression" in the same vein as do religious moralists who speak of "back-sliding." Both terms are used pejoratively and they both conceive of "losing ground." The pertinent paradigm is one which applies to certain board-games, in which one is subject to being sent back (by an opponent or by a fateful drawing) to "start." In that paradigm all the gained ground is indeed lost.

From the perspective of the human helix, one can move "in reverse" to any earlier point on the helical course, but the course itself remains intact, from "start" (birth) to the point of greatest advance. That means that the full course in any present moment is *familiar*, and therefore any part of it can be re-occupied with confidence and with rapid return.

A useful analogy for the paradigm of the human helix is that recognized in geographical exploration. When an explorer is on the frontier, he/she expects to eventually find a distant supply-station or to return to "base-camp" for supplies and provisions and fuel.

The pictorial representation of the human helix (Figs. 8 and 9) is probably obvious in its general structure, but there are

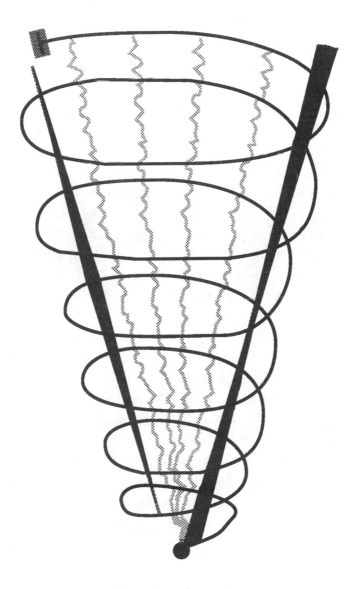

The Human Helix

component details which need explanation. The colors were chosen to represent specific functions and elements of the human helix.

In the side view (Fig. 8) you notice that there are two differently colored lateral "struts" which hold the helix in a stable shape. The blue color represents "positive" support — nurture, comfort, encouragement, empathy, safety, protection, refuge. Red (a warning color) represents the "negative" support of the False Self System which is included in every person's life course — controlling, molding, correcting, criticizing, monitoring, judging, odiously comparing, and punishing. In the ideal model which I have drawn notice that the blue support "strut" gets progressively wider. And the red "strut," which arises slightly later than the blue, enlarges as the person moves out into the socialized world in the teen-age years and beyond; then it gets progressively thinner as the person does her/his therapeutic work of dismantling and recovery.

The brown marker represents the most immediate "stuck point," a point at which there is not enough energy or motivation or information to continue a forward course. That point could be an interpersonal impasse, a physical illness, a difficult life-choice, or simply the common fatigue at the day's end.

Looking now at the top view (Fig. 9) of the helix, the prominent features are the brown marker and the blue and red "struts." Following the natural instructions of the True Self, the person will move "backwards" along his track until he finds support. "Positive" support is vastly preferable, but the familiar negative support of the False Self structure will suffice temporarily to re-fuel the person. The natural remedy for days-end fatigue is a good night's sleep — hardly a "regression" or a "backsliding," as the tyrants of the False Self System would charge.

For visual clarity only two "struts" were illustrated, but in point of fact every loop in the helical spiral is spangled with support-stations. Under stress or in fatigue or at an impediment one moves as quickly as possible to the nearest available adequate support-station. Human growth provides for a progressive increase in positive support and a progressive decrease in negative support.

The provision of the red "strut" in the helical model not only reminds us of the "good-hyphen-evil" nature of human life; it also is a corrective against the illusion of purity and perfectibility.

The thin green filaments are the upreaching light-seeking extensions from the True Self nucleus. They are the strands of nuclear distinctiveness (of individual uniqueness) which spread to infuse the Ego and the full Person. They also represent all the vital activity of inherent growth and of the healing systems (especially the immune-system).

A middle-aged woman recently reported a dream which, coupled with her waking associations, illustrates the natural movements "backwards" and "forwards" along her own self-inscribed helix. It also illustrates the "green-filament" creativity that characterizes the human unconscious.

The dream: "I was hanging on to the side of a locomotive which was going straight up into the air very fast; there were no tracks. There was no engineer inside and no passengers. But there was a man hanging onto the train just in front of me. I recognized him as a man I know in real life. He's gay and he used to be a friend, but I found out he's been laughing at me behind my back. Anyway, the train suddenly leveled off and stopped in a town. Jim, the man, told me we had come here to visit a friend of his. We left the locomotive. Hmm! I noticed I said "locomotive: again — I never use that word for "train" — I wonder what that's about?

We went to the door of his friend's house. As soon as the man came to greet us I realized he was Jim's lover. The man was rude to me and told me to wait in a back room while he and Jim made love. I felt confused and frightened, so I just did what he told me. I noticed a small window in my room that looked into another room like a nursery. I peeped in and saw three babies in a big crib. I knew they were triplets but somehow the boy was older than his two sisters. And I could tell by the expression on his face that he was trying to decide which of the sisters he would have sex with first. I knew I had to get out of there."

"I ran out of the house toward the train station. I was crying because I didn't have any money to buy a ticket. But just then I remembered that I've always kept two bills in a secret pocket of my billfold. I felt relieved on the train ride home because it was "on the level" and I knew I could get a fresh start in life."

Among the many striking aspects of this dream the one that most caught my attention was her use of the term "locomotive" which she registered as unusual. In dream-life the "unusual," unlike the bizarre, is generally a lodestar. I inquired about her use of the word and she repeated it several times. (This woman, parenthetically, had no formal education beyond the seventh grade but she is extremely bright and she has been a voracious reader of classical literature and especially of psychological theory throughout her adult life.) She suddenly broke the word in two, "loco-motive," and she burst out laughing.

"That's what that dream is about, isn't it?" It's telling me about the "loco" motives in my lifestyle. I've used sex all my life to get jobs and relationships — and that *is* a "loco" motive. And my connection with Jim was so typical — I originally befriended him because he was manic-depressive. I've been running around taking care of sick people who don't want to get well instead of taking care of myself — and that's the most "loco" motive of all, isn't it?"

The woman (who had been named Brigit because her mother "wanted her to grow up to look like Brigitte Bardot") grew reflective as she smiled softly.

"I was thinking about that locomotive going straight up and I was remembering what you told me once about the vertical and horizontal dimensions and I suddenly flashed back to my favorite day-dream when I was a teenager. I would imagine that I was the youngest member of an archaeology team digging for treasure in Egypt. The leader of the expedition was a much older man and very kind and I was his favorite, but none of the others were jealous of me. The leader and I had sex often but it was no big deal; it was just sweet and loving. And all the people on -the team were real kind. There was an older woman-member who would always bring me a cool Coca-Cola when I got hot digging. I believe that day-dream was about my real-self and then I got off the track. I think I'm getting back on. I'm digging again." She laughed with delight.

This lovely restitutional association which came up from Brigit's remembered past illustrates the principle of moving "backwards" along one's helical path until solid ground or ample support is found. There are other implications about the nature of the healthy helix as well.

Brigit's reference to my "teachings" about the vertical and the horizontal was quite apt. The energy of the Self unmodified by the Ego tends to move "vertically," that is between Heaven and Hell, between mania and depression, between creativity and inertia, between identity with God and identity with the Devil. The horizontal dimension in human consciousness relates to the object-relating orientation, that is to that of the Ego. And the energy of the Ego which is not balanced by narcissistic self-interest moves horizontally toward over-involvement with the environment, especially the interpersonal environment, or toward exhausted withdrawal. And that unmodified Ego energy also imposes either syrupy salvation or punitive reform on society.

In the loco mentality of the Christian West, the "vertical" and the "horizontal" are quite literally at cross purposes, and an artificial separation between "sacred" and "secular" is inevitable.

In the context of the artificial split between Self and Ego, re-examine the assumptions of the False Self System models. Notice that all of those models promise a deferred reward of Self-realization (of "getting to Heaven") by undergoing the trials of the flesh (the Ego). In the Progress Model one gets to the "landing" (the restful Heaven) by steadily climbing the steps of the societal staircase. In the Puritan Model one gets to course's end (the righteous Heaven) by avoiding error through the policing of the (Super) Ego. And in the Heroic Model one achieves victory (the triumphant Heaven) by heroically overcoming the odds or by heroically submitting to them.

Religious leaders urge us to get the "vertical" and the "horizontal" together, and that is a necessary urging if the two have indeed been split. The Christian symbolists find it especially convenient that the vertical and the horizontal convene in the Cross.

But in the perspectives of the Eastern philosophies and of the indigenous people there is no split into vertical and horizontal. Rather, for them, upreach and outreach are always simultaneous and co-existent. The assertion that "Everything is sacred" is the basic reality and not some pantheistic sop.

The configuration of the human helix conforms to the open-system perspective. Both the horizontal loops and the vertical struts and filaments co-exist at every moment. Vertical and horizontal meet (they "kiss," as in Psalm 85) but they do not intersect and form a cross. In the helical reality there is no irretrievable "error," so there is more a sense of opportunity than of urgency. Choices in the open system are between this life-or-that life rather than between life and death. In the True Self configuration of the Helix the choice of the moment is not crucial and life therefore is not excruciating.

The model of the Human Helix satisfies the characteristics of human growth in an open-system. However, like the False Self model, it does not include the final life-event which is Death.

I think it is not an accidental oversight that my models do not include Death. I have been raised in the Christianized industrialized nature-conquering Western World, and we of that world were taught to deny Death or to tolerate its prospect in hope of eternal life.

Just recently I was introduced to a model which complements and, I believe, completes the life-course model of the human helix. It is the living symbol (analogous perhaps to the Cross in Christianity) of the Tohono O'Odham Nation (Fig. 10).

This nation, formerly known by the Spanish-imposed name Papago, occupies a large reservation on inhospitable land in the

The Man In The Maze

far southhwest corner of Arizona.

The mythical father of the Tohono O'Odham ("The People of the Desert") is known as I'itoi. He came from a holy mountain to tell the people "how life was" and how it was to be lived. He showed them the Maze, which is "how life is." At the center of the maze is the starting point (birth) and the ending point (death); it is the same central point. There are no wrong turns in the maze, only different areas of exploration. And according to I'itoi, whose symbol came to be called "the Man in the Maze," one is to honor Death and to anticipate it positively. And although Death is a "good thing," the Creator, according to I'itoi, knew that people would still be fearful when they finally peered into the darkness at the center. So the kindly Creator fixed a small peninsula extending out from the center. The fearful and reluctant person facing Death can move onto that perch and stay as long as he wants to, looking back over his journey through life until he is satisfied with it and then ready to re-enter the darkness from whence he came.

Apart from Tohono mythology, at the level of universal symbolism, I would understand the "central darkness" of the maze to represent not only birth and death, but all new growth and attachment and all separation and loss throughout life as well. Insight-attachment is a small birth, and separation-loss is a small death. The "peninsula of contemplation" is provided for those repetitive events as well. One needs to "perch" and review in order to assimilate and integrate.

In a final salute to the principle of balance, there is another observation about the complementary relationship between the helical model and the maze. The helical model issues from a study of Western civilization, whose genius and curse is *individualism*. The prominence of the support-structures in the helical model provides a corrective against an isolating individualism. From the other direction, the symbol of the maze arises from a *tribal* culture in which individual identity is subsumed under that of the group. I'itoi's maze is a study in solitary individual consciousness, a corrective against an unbalanced communalism.

Thus the life-course of the human animal. Born of earthly mother and returning to Mother Earth — always moving toward the light, between the darkness of the womb and the darkness of the tomb.

The smaller picture is a panorama of woundings and healings, of losses and enrichments. The larger picture is encompassed by the helix and the maze. Amazing!

References and Notes

(1)   Page 1   The Oxford Dictionary of Quotations; Oxford University Press; N.Y. 1980; page 550.

(2)   Page 7   From The New Revised Standard Version of the Bible as contained in the Episcopal Book of Common Prayer, Oxford University Press, N.Y. 1990.

(3)   Page 8   *Wisdomkeepers*; Beyond Words Publishing, Inc.; Hillsboro, Oregon, 1990, pp. 68-71.

(4)   Page 12   The Poetry of Robert Frost; ed. Edward Lathem; Holt, Rinehart and Winston; N.Y.; 1969.

(5)   Page 59   *General System Theory*; Ludwig von Bertalanffy; George Braziller, Inc.; N.Y.; 1975.

(6)   Page 80   Passivity: Schiff, J. and Schiff, A.; Transactional Analysis Journal 1:1; January 1971.

(7)   Page 93   *Shame and Pride*: Donald L. Nathanson; W.W. Norton, N.Y.; 1992. (*Note*: My statement that shame is not a natural affect would first appear to be at variance with Silvan Tomkins' affect theory, of which Nathanson is the chief expositor. I believe, with Tomkins, that shame is a pivotal attenuating defense which protects the human animal from affective flooding. However I disqualify shame as a natural psychosocial affect because it has no natural consummatory exchange, as in comfort-for-sadness, in the environment.)

(8) Page 95 Script Drama Analysis: Karpman, S.B.: Transactional Analysis Bulletin 7:26; April 1968.

(9) Page 101 *Transactional Analysis in Psychotherapy*: Berne, Eric; Grove Press Inc.; N.Y.; 1961.

(10) Page 110 *The Age of Anxiety*: Auden, W. H.; Random House, N.Y.; 1947; p. 134.

(11) Page 113 Diagnostic Criteria from DSM-III-R; American Psychiatric Association; Washington D.C.; 1988; pp. 216-217.

(12) Page 119 *Meetings With Time*: Dennis, Carl; Penguin Books, N.Y.; 1992.

(13) Page 144 *For Your Own Good*: Miller, Alice; Farrar, Straus, Giroux; N.Y. 1983; p. 247 ff.

(14) Page 148 *Introduction to the Work of Melanie Klein*; Hanna Segal; Basic Books, N.Y.; p. 93 ff.

(15) Page 153 The American Heritage Dictionary of the English Language; Houghton Mifflin Company; Boston; 1981.

(16) Page 160 Why Walk When You Can Fly: Mary Chapin-Carpenter; Why Walk Music; 1994.

(17) Page 164 Oxford Dictionary of Quotations; ibid.

Index

Books may be obtained by mail-order, by direct purchase from the author's office, or from selected bookstores. If purchasing directly from office at 206 Ridgecrest Drive, Chapel Hill, call ahead (919) 929-2700 to assure the presence of a staff person to serve you.

ORDER FORM
Mail to:
Medicine Wheel Publications
Timberlyne Station Box 16121
Chapel Hill, N.C. 27516-6121

Please send _____ copies
of *The Recovery of the True Self* to:

Name: _____

Address: _____

State, Zip: _____

Orders from individuals must be pre-paid by check or money-order. N.C. residents add 6% sales tax. Your check will be cashed *after* the order is mailed.

Book(s) @ $15.00 _____

Mailing @ $1.40 _____

Packaging @ $.60 _____

Sales Tax _____

Total: _____